D0021569

EXPOSE
YOURSELF

EXPOSE YOURSELF

Using the Power of
Public Relations
to Promote
Your Business
and Yourself

——

MELBA BEALS

Chronicle Books ▪ San Francisco

Printed in the United States of America.

Library of Congress Cataloging in Publication Data

Beals, Melba
        Expose yourself: using public relations to promote yourself and
your business / Melba Beals.
             p.   cm.
        ISBN 0-87701-585-6
        1. Public relations.   I. Title.
HD59.B36   1990
659.2–dc20   89-28995
                                                                        CIP

Editing: Carey Charlesworth
Book and cover design: Linda Herman + Company, San Francisco
Composition: Mark Woodworth Typography

Distributed in Canada by Raincoast Books, 112 East
Third Avenue, Vancouver, B.C. V5T 1C8

10 9 8 7 6 5 4 3 2 1

Chronicle Books
275 Fifth Street
San Francisco, California 94103

I DEDICATE THIS BOOK TO

My mother, Dr. Lois Pattillo,

and to

Kellie Beals

The Conrad Pattillo family

George and Carole McCabe

Alaister and Consi Smith

David Geissinger

Lynn Ludlow

Dorothy Divack

Mimi Silbert

David Keller

Patricia O'Neil

Millie and Edward Johnston

Cathy and Sanford Rosen and family

John and Maria Picard

Phyllis Westberg

Babette Wurtz

Contents

PART FOUR

PR Power in Action: Specific Strategies

PART FIVE

Evaluating Your PR Plans

Expose Yourself is for everyone
who wants to understand
the power of public relations.

Preface

My Venture into
Public Relations

My first experience of the power of the media came in 1957 when, as a sixteen-year-old, I was thrust center stage as one of nine black children who integrated Central High School in Little Rock, Arkansas. Under the protection of the Army's 101st Airborne Division I entered those halls and broke a Southern tradition.

Reporters gathered from everywhere. Only the day before I had been tucked away in my quiet, secluded space; now, in front of the whole world, I was sitting on the hot seat. Cameras. Lights. Action! The reporters were questioning me—little me. They wanted to know how I felt, what I did, and what I thought about being a tender warrior on the civil rights battlefield.

I was subjected to the closest scrutiny from the press and was forced to learn how to deal with the media in a professional manner. I was written about in nearly every major periodical in the world and featured in television news shows. The nine of us were voted the top news story of the year. A press conference a day, interviews, flashing cameras, and the pressure of live-action news formats all provided me with a speedy—and thorough—education in the media.

I credit the media with saving my life. The glare of photojournalists' lights had shown the world darkened corners where white-hooded men made evil plans to kill children. Amid violent mobs the news reporters stood like beacons of hope, emphasizing that justice is demanded when real Americans witness injustice. It is understandable that I would, as an adult, have a fascination for the media and become a news reporter.

When I was seventeen I started writing articles and publishing them in New York–based newspapers. I went on to earn a graduate degree from Columbia University's School of Journalism and to take my first media job as a reporter for KQED, a public broadcast television station in San Francisco. I later moved to KRON-TV, the San Francisco–based NBC station, where I worked as a reporter.

After seven years in broadcast journalism I began publishing articles in magazines, including *People* and *Essence,* and in other national and local periodicals. It was my way of making a transition; I could stay in the profession I loved and still have the flexibility that would allow me to become a better single parent.

Free-lance writing was stimulating and rewarding, but after a while I wanted more financial stability. My good friend Karolyn Rausche, a seasoned publicist herself, pointed out what suddenly became obvious: I had writing skills, knowledge of the media, solid contacts, and a real feel for the public relations industry. I was already acting as a publicist for many of my friends' ventures—why not get paid for it?

My first official client was famed international "Tort King" attorney Melvin Belli and his law firm. He is a promotional expert; for more than half a century he has used public relations to build a major national and international legal practice. Through my work with him I learned more about the power of public relations than I did from any of the university courses I'd taken. I learned the skill of generating media interest for almost any topic or event in any media market in the world. With only a moment's notice he would direct me to conduct a campaign in Germany, England, or France. "See that they know I'm coming, honey," he would say on his way out the door.

My list of clients grew, and I began handling specialized publicity campaigns for doctors, lawyers, image consultants, artists, creative-think geniuses, seminar speakers, psychologists, authors, and many other individuals, small businesses, and corporations.

Later, as Patricia Montandon started her worldwide peace pilgrimage with Children as the Peacemakers, traveling to China, Italy, West and East Germany, India, and repeatedly to Moscow, she enlisted my services to set up massive international publicity campaigns. I felt a strange sensation in my heart as I made three a.m. phone calls to newspapers in Beijing. "The blue folder!" I would yell into the telephone receiver, as if volume would make my words more understandable.

During the trip, Patricia would call from one of her outposts in Russia or China and say how happy she was to see one of my blue media packets in the hands of a smiling journalist. I got quite a thrill out of discovering just how well the system of disseminating information works no matter where one is on this planet.

Whatever the nature of the business—small or large, domestic or international—promotional activity is necessary. After more than twenty years of working in media dissemination I have distilled my experience, strategies, and insights into this book. Here is how to expose yourself for fun and profit.

Introduction

Whenever you are tempted to think a public relations campaign isn't going to do anything for you or your business, remember the Pet Rock caper.

Using a well-planned PR campaign, the creative inventor of the Pet Rock made us believe we needed to spend our hard-earned dollars on a piece of rock similar in size and description to any rock in our backyards. He lured us into stores to make that outrageous purchase while his bank balance climbed to the million-dollar mark.

What sold us on the Pet Rock? Public relations—all those intriguing, seductive tidbits employed by the creator of this little concept to get our attention. We found ourselves bombarded with talk about the Pet Rock on radio, on television, and in print. We responded to his PR campaign. He convinced us of the value of his product and we bought.

I'm not suggesting public relations is a tool that will enable you to sell an inferior product; word of mouth will quickly eliminate a product or service that lacks integrity. The Pet Rock creator told us exactly what he was offering and made no claims about what it could do for our sex lives, hair growth, job opportunities, or relationships.

My point is that he called a rock a rock and yet enticed us to buy it because he told us the truth in a way that titillated our fancies.

Is Publicity Really What You Need?

Maybe you have been under the impression that publicity is a frivolous pastime indulged in by large corporations with big budgets. But the conscientious exposure of one's self, one's service, or one's product to the buying public is a necessary task in these times of stiff competition. Perhaps there was a time when an excellent product resulted in a ready-made market because it was rare, new, and exciting. Those days are long gone.

With today's immediate imitations of absolutely every product or service, even a brilliant original cannot afford to wait for word of mouth to attract customers. The sheer numbers of similar businesses make it even more necessary for you to find a way of blowing your own horn and letting everyone know that what you have to offer is a cut above the rest. The growing emergence of businesses owned and operated by one person makes the market even more complex.

Estimates are that four out of five new businesses will fail before the end of their first year. Too often that failure occurs because the entrepreneur, intentionally or unintentionally, has kept the business a close little secret among select circles.

Those entrepreneurs who are unaware that publicity is a valuable partner will open their businesses and depend too heavily on the initial wave of support from friends and neighbors. As time passes, however, that support dwindles, and ill-conceived emergency promotional efforts fail to perk up a falling client response. Even with a successful start, over time a product or service will saturate a narrow market. The supply of customers is exhausted and you must find a way to get your message to a new universe, a fresh batch of folks who want to buy what you are selling. This is true even of businesses that have lots of repeat patronage, such as hair salons or grocery stores.

One way to continue to replenish your customer base is through publicity. Publicity that gets you and your product before the public and boosts sales—either long or short term—is a valuable business aid.

But not all publicity is beneficial. No doubt you've heard the old adage "There's no such thing as bad publicity," or "Spell my name wrong but at least spell it." Perhaps this philosophy is true in some cases—negative publicity about the spicy passages in a book or the raunchy scenes in a movie can mean more sales. But bad publicity surrounding a product or service can indeed cast a shadow. For example, millions of dollars of advertising cannot obliterate the image in the minds of many people that a deranged person put poison in a particular brand of headache capsule.

Take care with your product or service. Be certain that what you offer for sale, what you want to publicize, can stand up to public scrutiny.

You should also realize that access to the media is a privilege you will have only as long as you respect it and take responsibility for the duties accompanying its use.

Becoming Your Own Publicist

Expose Yourself is designed to guide you, step by step, through the process of conducting your own public relations campaign. With the proper use of the instructions you will be able to gain access to the media and garner thousands of dollars in free publicity for you, your product or service.

This book is a savvy guide for small-business owners who want to increase sales through increased public awareness of their product; doctors or lawyers who want to build lucrative practices; authors who want to promote their books; nonprofit groups that want to maintain high public profiles for fund-raising; individuals who want to get their point of view across to the public; and anyone who wants to disseminate information about the value of their service or product.

Expose Yourself provides an easily comprehensible view of what public relations is and how you can use it. The easy-to-follow instructions enable you to write your own press releases, execute media mailings, and pitch your story to producers and editors. You will learn the secrets of planning an event, framing an issue to attract reporters and cameras, and presenting yourself most favorably on a talk show or during an interview.

If you prefer to have a professional handle your publicity campaign, *Expose Yourself* will provide you with the knowledge to formulate your goals effectively and to hire the right publicist.

This book will also enable you to recognize when you are the target of a campaign aimed at attracting your attention, garnering your vote, swaying your opinion, or getting your dollar.

Expose Yourself is for everyone who wants to understand and harness the power of public relations.

PART ONE

The Power of
Public Relations

1

Discovering Public Relations

If you count on the public to purchase your product or service and you are not getting the success you desire, develop your PR power. Skilled use of PR power—public relations campaigns—can provide an opportunity to sell to hundreds, if not thousands, of people at one time. Newspapers, magazines, radio, and television all provide access to the buying public, your potential customers. Public relations is an enormously valuable way to use the media to your advantage. You can catapult products, people, and services into the spotlight. When you convince the public you offer a product or service that fills their needs, your sales volume will soar.

How Other People's PR Power Pushes Your Buy Buttons

You respond to publicity campaigns every day; other people's PR power sways your opinions, often without your being conscious of it. Consider the sources of information that dictated some of your most recent purchases.

That latest self-help book you are reading, for example: Where did you get the idea to buy it? Were you influenced by the dapper, fatherly gentleman whose face and voice you recognized? Did his personal story of how he changed and organized his life persuade you to purchase? You probably made the expenditure because a "media friend," one you know and trust, testified to its value.

The car you drive, the neighborhood you live in, the clothing you wear, the physical fitness center you frequent, the magazines you read—all these are choices influenced by subtle bits of information from the media. If you doubt my assertion, begin to examine the areas in your life where you have had an opinion altered by a newspaper article, a book or movie review, or a TV or radio talk show. You will be amazed at the role publicity plays in your life.

If you are part of a working couple with children, operating on a tight schedule with little time for pondering purchases, PR power is likely a helpful shopping companion. It exposes you to innovative advances in safe toys, computer software, nutritional food, and easy-care clothing.

We allow ourselves to be persuaded by these promotional campaigns because we have neither the time nor the energy to conduct, firsthand, the kind of comparative research needed to make sensible choices. So we succumb to publicity, first trying one suggestion, then making a second selection if the product or service fails to live up to claims made.

Begin keeping track of the stories in the features section of your newspaper that mention particular salons, restaurants, physical fitness centers, or shoppers' havens. They were, no doubt, generated by some clever business owner or publicist as part of a well-planned publicity campaign aimed at attracting your attention and getting you to buy whatever they have to offer.

Notice how often you are tempted to alter a decision to purchase, merely because you have been seduced by PR power. When you become aware of the role promotional campaigns play in your life and realize how many times they push your "buy" buttons, you will understand how you can use that same PR power to activate your customers' buttons.

2

PR Power:
Your Key to Success

The appropriate promotional campaign can be a key that opens many doors to success for you and your business. It can generate immediate financial gain while building long-term enhancement of your public image.

PR Is an Affordable Business Aid

Most small-business owners search for an inexpensive shot in the arm that will yield immediate results. They seldom have enough money to invest the $20,000 or more that it costs to mount the first phase of a productive local advertising campaign. A four-by-five-inch ad printed one time only in a local newspaper with a hundred fifty thousand readers currently costs an average of $3,000. A strip of five thirty-second radio ads in an average-sized city can cost $2,000 or more. A modest ad campaign can easily cost at least $50,000.

PR power is an effective sales booster for small-business owners because budget limitations need not dictate the level of success of a public relations campaign. With paper, a word processor or typewriter, stamps, and the willingness to invest old-fashioned elbow grease, a small-business owner can get off to a good start. Self-promoters have begun their campaigns with a $250 budget combined with their own creative energy and chutzpah. They have executed smashing publicity campaigns that brought them thousands of dollars in free media exposure and an immediate increase in sales.

One of the negative voices in your head may be saying that you can't do it yourself because you don't know anybody in the media. Yes, of course it helps if you know the media decision makers or have a brother whose dogcatcher is related to the street sweeper whose uncle is on the evening news. And yes, that is one of the selling points publicists offer. They have connections to the "right people." However, a lack of connections does not preclude your having that same access.

During the years I worked as a television news reporter perhaps one third of the stories broadcast had been covered because someone at the station had personal knowledge of the individual or organization requesting coverage. It was a unique quirk in a story presentation and media release, coupled with well-thought-out telephone marketing, that usually attracted the assignment editor's attention. Like all working people, news reporters and assignment editors under deadline pressure must often make decisions based purely on what is expedient. Media releases facilitate coverage by giving them the facts and figures in a neat package. A well-written media release is your vehicle for getting the media exposure you seek.

Of course, if you have connections in the media—and almost everybody knows somebody—certainly do not overlook them. They can be an added bonus.

The Financial Benefits of PR Power

The financial benefits of PR power can be measured in two ways. The first is the direct return in free exposure; the second is sales to customers. It is not unreasonable to expect an upswing in sales in response to even the first media appearance.

A few years ago, two women invested $6,000 to hire a publicist to promote their newly opened business. They enjoyed a return of more than $60,000 in free advertising, along with a twenty percent increase in their sales volume. Their story is simple.

These women had become instant entrepreneurs as a creative response to their midlife crises. They opened a small specialized San Francisco gallery displaying and selling giant objets d'art: you've no doubt seen their eight-foot-tall plastic toothbrushes or the six-foot-high pencils. The initial task was to make themselves and their products appealing to the public. Their personal stories worked well as a hook to attract media interest.

After the distribution of media packets to local outlets, numerous phone calls were made to sell the women's story to the electronic and print media. In order to provide more points of interest for the media the story pointed to three local celebrities who were displaying the objects in their homes. Television producers were even more delighted with this pretty picture story.

The results were smashing. Both the women and their merchandise were televised in a seven-minute TV magazine segment that aired on "Evening Magazine" locally and in other cities. Local newspaper editors were intrigued by the midlife-crisis angle as well as by the look of the objects. One story was picked up by the wire services and transmitted to newspapers across the country.

Word of the unique shop reached Canadian and Japanese newspapers, bringing queries from foreign visitors and volumes of mail orders. Long after the main thrust of the publicity campaign had subsided the women continued to enjoy its reflected benefits.

If these women had started with the skill and desire to wage their own promotional campaign instead of hiring a publicist they could have done so with an investment of as little as $500 for materials, along with the expenditure of their own time and energy. They chose to put their talents into other aspects of their business.

Advertising versus PR Power: A What-If Discussion

Let us compare the differences in the costs of promotional campaigns and direct advertising. Assume you are the owner of a small cafe. You have set aside a budget of $500 to promote your business during the year. You elect to spend your money on a four-by-five-inch ad in your local newspaper. It appears one time only. Within the available space, the ad extols the virtues of your cafe. You elect to highlight your exotic one-of-a-kind menu, the exquisite ambiance, and convenient location. You include a coupon offering new visitors a twenty-percent discount on their meal.

During the first few days following the ad's appearance you revel in the ring of your cash register, blissfully basking in the overflow lunch crowd. Two weeks later, however, you realize the bunch for lunch has dwindled to a precious few. You may even be right back to the original crowd with an additional one or two newcomers. Tallying up the monies earned from what you believe to be direct responses to the ad, you generously estimate $500. Now what?

You have spent $500 to earn $500. The question is, do you now take out ads on a continuous basis? The results don't warrant it. You realize it will take a sustained promotional campaign over time to make a positive difference in your business. You find yourself in a quandary.

Activating your PR power is the answer. You must create and conduct your own promotional campaign. It can become a consistent and affordable method not only for attracting but also for holding new customers. If you are willing to invest the time and energy required to perfect this skill, it will serve you well.

What if instead of advertising you spend $250 of your budget on paper, printing, and mailing a one-page media release showcasing the fascinating details of your eatery's history. You reveal your unique approach to nutritious but elegant and low-cost meals. You follow your media mailing with phone calls—telemarketing—to producers and editors, extolling the restaurant's ambiance and unique menu.

In response to your campaign you receive two radio and one television appearances in the first month. The direct advertising dollar value of that media exposure is $5,000. Following one television appearance you are asked to speak about your business before the Rotary Club. You begin to experience a steady increase in customers over a three-month period and you add a table in the corner for the burgeoning lunch crowd. With a little strategizing, you continue to get requests for public appearances.

Six months later, if there is a lull in your appearance requests, you can use your remaining $250 for a second media mailing. You reframe your pitch to producers and editors, varying your approach from the first one. Perhaps you decide to associate yourself with a favored community charity. You focus on additional and different media outlets than before.

Your $500 budget has brought you media exposure, public recognition, and a sustained increase in business. At the same time, your efforts will have enhanced your image within your community.

Long-Term Benefits of PR Power

Each additional media appearance, if done properly, is a building block for your promotional campaign, a foundation on which you will be able to expand your business. As the PR momentum builds, producers and editors become familiar with you, and you develop ties and even some friendships within the media while also creating alliances with various community groups. Through these pipelines you communicate with even more people, who begin to know and trust you. These new customers become comfortable with you and your service or product, and of course they tell their friends. Your PR power will have become an invaluable long-term business aid.

Do You Want to Do It Yourself?

Whether you have realized it or not, you have been running your own personal public relations agency since birth. No doubt you began as a toddler persuading your parents of your personal attributes and achievements in order to be allowed to play with the neighborhood kids or your favorite tricycle. In grammar school you promoted yourself to your teachers, to fellow classmates, and to members of teams or organizations you wanted to join.

As you moved through your teen years you learned how to sell yourself to that girl or boy you wanted to take to the school dance. Whether you used subtle campaigns, paraded through the school yard with a banner, or pitted yourself against the school bully to show off your strength, you were publicizing what you had to offer.

The question that remains is, are you ready to polish these PR skills so they bring you sales and money?

ASSESSING YOUR PR RESOURCES

1. What is your immediate budget for publicizing your business?
   - ☐ less than $500
   - ☐ $500 to $1,000
   - ☐ $1,000 to $3,000
   - ☐ $3,000 to $10,000
   - ☐ $10,000 to $20,000

2. Are you able to spend eight hours per week publicizing your business?
   - ☐ yes
   - ☐ no

3. How do you assess your telephone personality?
   - ☐ excellent
   - ☐ wonderful
   - ☐ good
   - ☐ so-so
   - ☐ awful
   - ☐ I hate talking on the telephone

4. Do you have any experience at selling?
   - ☐ yes
   - ☐ no

5. Your business is
   - ☐ new
   - ☐ six months old
   - ☐ a year old
   - ☐ two years old or older

6. Are you willing to expose yourself—to be a star—and appear on the airwaves or in print to talk about your service or product?
   - ☐ yes
   - ☐ no

7. If your business includes more than one person, is there an employee who could support you in your PR effort?
   - ☐ yes
   - ☐ no

8. How effective are you in coordinating detailed assignments?
   - ☐ very
   - ☐ adequate
   - ☐ poor

9. Have you any experience at conducting a publicity campaign or marketing a product or service?
   - ☐ yes
   - ☐ no

10. Are you convinced about your urgent need for publicizing your business? Are you passionate about the endeavor? Do you believe in your heart it is a worthwhile investment of your time, energy and money?
    - ☐ yes
    - ☐ no

11. Do you have a compelling drive to make a success of your business venture?
    - ☐ yes
    - ☐ no

12. Are you willing to go all out, to be outrageous if necessary? Are you willing to fail, then alter your course of action to achieve your goals?
    - ☐ yes
    - ☐ no

It is necessary to make a realistic appraisal of your present stance in order to determine whether you have what it takes to excel as your own publicist. If you doubt your response to any of the questions in the Assessing Your PR Resources questionnaire, ask the opinion of someone close to you.

If you are in the very beginning stages of a business that takes all of your time and you are already exhausted, then it is not reasonable to assume you can add yet another task to your burden. If, however, you can spend eight hours a week publicizing your business, then your time allocation is within the norm: for every forty hours worked, eight should be spent getting new customers.

Suppose you answer "awful" to the telephone question, number three. Worse, you absolutely hate telephones, don't like gabbing with people, and never have a smile in your voice. Abandon any idea of doing your own public relations. Half the effort of any publicity campaign is time spent on the telephone. If you are unable to commandeer your spouse, lover, or employee to take over this task you will fail at activating your PR power.

If you have a good telephone manner but no experience in selling, you can learn to telemarket. It is a skill that is explained in Chapter Eight.

Question seven is an important one. If you are shy and unwilling to take the spotlight, unwilling to expose yourself, you need to consider just who you want to represent you and your business. It must be someone who is articulate, with an appealing appearance and manner. The person must, above all else, understand your business profile and philosophy. (See Chapter Nineteen: Hiring an Outside Publicist.)

Another crucial issue: if there is more than one business owner there is sometimes more than one huge ego to deal with. In other words, does everybody want to be a star? That question must be thrashed out before you begin. Which of you is best suited to function as the publicist, and which at taking the limelight? We're all stars, you say? Well then, you'll need to decide which one is the predominant star. Hitch your wagon to one and only one, allowing the others to function as alternates. Draw straws or behave as rational adults. Decide who best represents the business image; choose with dignity. And yes, there are instances in which all of you will be in the spotlight, but often periodicals or shows want to interview only one person.

If you've never been involved in a publicity campaign, answering no to question nine, then ask other people for their experiences. Chances are your friends have been involved in one and can discuss what it feels like to be caught up in the momentum. Once you become conscious of them you will note that publicity campaigns are going on all around you. A lack of experience is not a major detriment if you are willing to observe. If one of your friends is having a press conference, attend it.

Questions ten through twelve are important because they assess your commitment. You should have a passionate desire to become your own publicist. A half-hearted pitch on the telephone will net you a half-hearted response from the media. The decision makers will be just as enthusiastic about your story as you are.

Even if you have negative answers to all these questions, keep reading. By the end of the book you may have generated enthusiasm. Activating your own PR power gives a sense of accomplishment and satisfaction!

3

Activating Your PR Power

The first step in becoming your own publicist is to familiarize yourself with your customers in order to view your business from their perspective. Take a thorough inventory of each aspect of what you offer, weighing advantages and disadvantages. Your task is to create ways to communicate to potential customers the assets that set you apart from your competitors.

Effective marketing of a product or service includes product, price, and location as well as promotional opportunities. It is the fine tuning of these areas—the quality of your product or service, your pricing structure in respect to the market, your location, and how you choose to promote what you are selling—that brings together the kind of package that is appealing to customers.

Become your own customer. Define, in writing, the positive aspects of your product or service. What are the negative aspects? How does what you offer compare with similar products or services?

Shop around; survey your competitors. Select the best of what's available at the most reasonable prices. Where does your product or service rank on the totem pole? Would you buy what you are selling? Would you choose your product above all others as being the most cost effective?

An inventory like the accompanying Comparative Evaluation will yield positive results if you dare to be brutally honest. Clarifying the comparative value of your product or service will help you make your promotional campaign more effective. Through this comparison you will discern which aspects of your business to emphasize—you will know precisely why a customer should choose what you are selling.

Who Are Your Customers?

A thorough understanding of present customers will enable you to seek and seduce new buyers through your public relations campaign. Devise a customer profile (see Customer Profile questionnaire page 15) that spe-

COMPARATIVE EVALUATION

Three competitors who offer virtually the same product or service as I do are

_____

_____

_____

Comparing my prices with those of my competitors, I rank
- ☐ slightly lower   ☐ about the same   ☐ much higher
- ☐ slightly higher   ☐ much lower

The quality of my product or service compares with my competitors' as
- ☐ about the same   ☐ more value   ☐ less value

Advantages offered by my competitors that I fail to offer are

_____ _____

_____ _____

_____ _____

_____ _____

Were I shopping for the product or service I offer, I would choose to purchase it from_____

One good promotional approach used by my competitors to attract customers is

_____

One thing I could do to improve my product or service in comparison with my competitors' would be to_____

One group of customers overlooked by my competitors that I attract is

_____

The one thing I could do to be more competitive immediately is

_____

cifies why buyers choose your product or service. Is it the extraordinary quality of your product or service? Is it your proximity to their residence or work? Is it their special need for your unique product that makes them purchase? Is it your pricing structure? What combination of these reasons causes customers to choose to patronize your business?

Being aware of the lifestyles and buying habits of present and potential customers provides you with valuable information about how and where to contact them. Most businesses divide customers into three main categories: primary customers, who buy most often; secondary customers, who buy less frequently; and tertiary customers, who buy only now and then. You must recognize the differences between these people's propensities to purchase what you are selling and why they fall into the categories they do.

Naturally, primary customers are the core of your buying force. They usually live or work close by or perhaps pass your business on their daily travels. Their reason for purchasing may also be that they have a special need you alone can fill; hence they are willing to travel across town to buy your one-of-a-kind widget.

Secondary customers purchase less often but on a consistent basis over time. They may live outside your immediate area or have a less urgent need for what you offer.

Tertiary customers purchase sporadically. As you identify these last two groups of people you will begin to understand how to increase their interest in your product or service. Discover why and how they patronize your business. Find out what it would take from you to transform the second- and third-level purchasers into primary customers.

Survey your customers' opinions by devising a questionnaire that allows them to give you anonymous feedback. Don't be afraid of criticism, keeping in mind that most people like to feel that their comments—negative or positive—are listened to. Within the survey create opportunities for positive testimonies acknowledging the high quality of your product or service; you can use these responses to attract more customers.

Once you have a thorough understanding of your customer profiles you will be able to schedule media appearances or plan stories that will reach each target group, perhaps simultaneously. Knowing what appeals to them means you can push the buy buttons of hundreds, if not thousands, of people with one appearance on a drive-time radio show or a morning magazine television show. Your degree of success will be contingent on your willingness to maintain a meticulous record of their purchasing patterns.

It is paramount that you keep detailed records of your customers' patronage and that you update those files on a regular basis.

CUSTOMER PROFILE

According to my records _____ people have purchased my service/product over the past _____ years.

Those who most often purchase are ☐ males or ☐ females whose ages range from _____ to _____

Most of my customers work in these professions: _____

_____

Most of my customers read _____ (name of newspaper)
watch _____ (names of television shows)
watch the news on channel _____
listen to _____ (names of radio shows).

Most of my customers live in the _____ area.

Most of my customers' yearly salaries range from _____ to _____

My customers first used my service/product because they heard about it from

_____

The level of most of my customers' education is _____

My customers tend to lean toward _____ in their political beliefs.

A common characteristic of those who choose my service is _____

_____

Most of my customers are ☐ married ☐ single ☐ divorced.

The last four people who chose to partake of my service/product say they did so because _____

_____

The reason given most often for buying what I sell is _____
_____

The reason I expected to be given most often for buying what I sell is _____
_____

One place most of my customers frequent is _____

One event I could plan that would bring together most of my customers, past and
present, would be _____

Many of my customers attend the following: _____
_____
_____

I perceive my customers' needs as	I offer these skills and services
_____	_____
_____	_____
_____	_____
_____	_____
_____	_____

My skills and services meet my customers' needs by	Ways I don't meet my customers' needs but might do so in the future
_____	_____
_____	_____
_____	_____
_____	_____
_____	_____

An effective promotional campaign communicates to your customers how what you are selling meets their needs. Unless you are certain of the significance of what you offer and how it links to a need, you won't be able to describe it.

Painting an Appropriate Self-Portrait

Once you thoroughly understand your customers' points of view you are prepared to polish your image. Refining your view of what you are offering will help you convey to others an appealing written or verbal self-portrait. As a beginning exercise, fill out the Self-Evaluation questionnaire (page 18).

One illuminating way to analyze your present business image is to pretend your business is a person. Every business has a distinct personality. Knowing what gender, style, and posture best represents your business will help you present it to others.

Were your business a person, would it be masculine or feminine? How is that person dressed: in a pinstripe suit or Yves Saint Laurent evening gown? Is this person carrying a briefcase or a beaded purse? Is the mood carefree or serious? Is the person at work or at play? Is the person politically liberal or conservative? What is unique about the person's philosophical point of view? What colors best reflect the mood of your business? Will it be bright, cheery yellows, greens, or reds, or alluring, sophisticated tones of mauve and brown? Would your person be more aptly clothed in hues of gray or navy?

Once you develop these concepts you can use them to set tones that will be reflected throughout your promotional materials.

An example of how the process works can be seen in the promotional campaign of a financial counselor. This type of business is generally perceived as masculine, whether the owner is male or female. We as a society still regard any service or product that has to do with structure or form as being masculine. A financial counselor is expected to be precise, strong, decisive, stable, and self-assured: everyone wants to believe that strength and structure guide the services of financial counselors. Consequently, hues of peach and violet, soft colors that signal passive qualities, would not project the desired image.

No matter what style is portrayed by the written words in the promotional materials, it is likely that pastel colors would override any images in the recipient's mind. The thematic plotting of your business image should be consistent in text and illustration and in color and texture for all materials and presentations.

You should paint your promotional portrait in persuasive and compelling language. Use descriptive phrases. Note that highly technical language and complex explanations are reader turn-offs.

Everybody Is a Star

Your product is not exotic, you protest. People will be bored, you lament. Not true. Absolutely every product or person can be promoted. It is up to you to create an irresistible promotional strategy.

Ten words that describe the ways in which I serve clients or customers are

_____   _____

_____   _____

_____   _____

_____   _____

_____   _____

If my closest friend visited my business, I would sell him or her my service or product   ☐ without reservation   ☐ with only a little reservation
☐ with stark fear

What I sell   ☐ is my personal best   ☐ has room for improvement
☐ is good enough for the market

Three ways in which I could improve my product or service are _____

_____

_____

If I were giving superior service to my customers I would be _____

_____

When I meet a stranger, I explain my product or service in these twenty-five words or fewer: _____

_____

_____

If my business were a person, its personality could be described as
☐ sparkling   ☐ stoic   ☐ dynamic   ☐ distinctive   ☐ ordinary   ☐ other

I could service _____ new customers this month if I would_____

_____

I last surveyed my customers' likes/dislikes about my product or service on_____

Here's an example: a man wrote a book on creative thinking. There are dozens of such books and, indeed, the topic has been overdone. This gentleman, however, a dignified Ph.D., dared to risk presenting himself in a flamboyant manner. He made his media debut on a morning television show wearing a three-piece suit and a dunce cap. The first words out of his mouth were, "I'm allowing myself to be a dunce so I have the freedom to create another outrageous million-dollar idea. You, too, can be a millionaire if you are willing to risk behaving like a dunce! Each of you has a million-dollar idea. You're just too frightened of being a dunce to let it out."

Audience attention was riveted to his presentation. Who would dare to turn the dial?

This author was obeying the cardinal rule of a promotional campaign: don't be boring! The fastest road to disaster and anonymity in media is a dull, unimaginative presentation. When the word gets around, you won't even be able to get a seat in the audience of your favorite talk show. Be creative! Be ludicrous! But, for gosh sake, don't be boring.

Going back to the example of the financial consultant, if this entrepreneur gives a lengthy description of available services without showcasing the details in an appealing context, the presentation will be boring. But what if the person conveys the message that he or she can assist you in budgeting your way to early retirement or to that dream vacation you've wanted or the sports car you've been coveting. Suppose services are touted as a quick route to luxurious retirement or worry-free survival in tight times. How about a financial consultant that promises to help customers acquire all the basics you need and the luxuries you want.

Another appealing approach might be simply to say that this consultant can make you feel good about the way you spend your money. This kind of comfortable appeal would attract customers to explore the notion of being at ease about money—something few working people experience.

A person organizing a new cleaning service could describe himself as a housekeeper, a domestic wizard, or a housewife's dream. Which one would you choose?

A gentleman showed up at my door telling me he was a lifestyle facilitator. He had reference letters written by two of my friends. He promised that his joy would be to "move me through the cleaning experience without trauma."

Presenting his business profile with dignity and flair, this person enthralled me with his promotion. I hired him on the spot.

Although there was really nothing special about his cleaning service, he had an abundance of customers. He took the time to discern customer needs and to bone up using the least hint I gave him about something that concerned or interested me. He owed his success to his ingenuity and pride of workmanship. He turned what was for most a mundane job into the lot of a prince. Believe me, when he departed to go back to medical school, I was hard put to replace him. His other clients mourned him with equal fervor.

Any promotional writing should put your product or service in a similar light by explaining how what you are offering will enhance customers' lives. People are willing to spend their money on products and services they feel will improve the quality of their lives.

Knowing your product and your customer is the key to successful promotion of your business.

4

Your Customers Are Everywhere

There is a money tree right in your own backyard. It's true—there are clients all around you, whatever your lifestyle.

There are clients where you worship, at the grocery store, at your tennis club, in your Tai Chi class, at your dentist's office, on the bus, even in your neighborhood community meetings. If you've been hiding, shy about saying who you are and what you do, now is the time to come out of the closet.

How about starting with those clients right at your fingertips? Look in your Rolodex: are there any former clients listed? How long since you've telephoned to talk about what they are doing now and how your present services might fit their needs? More than likely a "new" client is already in your files: someone who has enjoyed the privilege of experiencing your high-quality product or service is the best candidate to purchase once more.

Friends are a major source of business. How many of your friends and acquaintances have you talked to about what you offer and how it might meet their needs? Do you realize that by not doing so you might be depriving them of something they desperately need? Because you haven't told them of the superior quality of your product or service they might have chosen an inferior one offered by your competitor.

Prospecting among organizations and clubs in your area can be fun. Pick a group—Women Entrepreneurs, Young Men Executives, Yoga Experts of America, Caterers over Thirty, it makes little difference what the organization—even your local YMCA or YWCA uses speakers for certain occasions. Offer your services; tell them what topic you can speak about and how it can benefit the audience.

Check your community phone directory or leaf through your Chamber of Commerce list of community organizations. Pick ten organizations that might be interested in what you are offering and volunteer yourself as an expert speaker.

Where do you purchase groceries? Tell the grocer about the availability of your product or service. Could you leave fliers or samples? How about your laundry or cleaners? Take your brochure.

When meeting friends for golf, take along a business card. During your iced-tea break, start a conversation that creates an opportunity for you to talk about the unique aspects of your business. Do you work out at a gym? Always have those business cards tucked into your sweat suit. Have a personal goal of meeting two new people each visit and, of course, tell them about your offering.

Whatever charity or volunteer organization you support, you have the chance to contribute your business services in a way that will yield fruit. Seize those prime opportunities to speak to all the members about your work and to make them aware that your talents as an accountant, illustrator, or whatever are available outside the organization.

Are you a member of a social club? Have you inquired whether any member needs your services? During casual conversation, have you sought to explain your business services?

Within any organization you join there are always opportunities to attract new clients. Invite members of your organization to take a tour of your attractive, appealing company. Is it too small? Then have a series of small gatherings on a regular basis for the purpose of "getting to know each other." During those gatherings and at other times give away coupons for half an hour of free consultation or a special sample of your product. Have an open house especially geared to interest members of your organization. If you have offices or a plant that has extra space, fix up the room and offer it as a meeting place for community groups.

Are you a parent? What about members of the PTA, parents of your child's playmates, your pediatrician, or anyone who currently delivers a service to your child?

Your favorite avocation or hobby, no matter what it is, presents opportunities for you to conduct business. "Lifetrack" public relations is the process of being willing to tell everyone you meet that you and your business exist, that you are special, and that you have something of value to offer. No matter who you are or what you do, creating an ongoing pattern of PR will enable you to find clients.

The Customer Development questionnaire (page 23) enables you to track your possibilities for clients. As you fill it in you'll be amazed at the opportunities you have passed up.

Analyze your personal address book. Are there contacts you've overlooked among old friends? Have you told those friends you are searching for new business? Often the most difficult task is to verbalize a need to a

CUSTOMER DEVELOPMENT

Places of business I visit once a week: Potential contacts:

_____ _____
_____ _____
_____ _____
_____ _____
_____ _____
_____ _____

Places of business I frequent
once a day: Potential contacts:

_____ _____
_____ _____
_____ _____
_____ _____
_____ _____

Personal services I regularly use: Potential contacts:

_____ _____
_____ _____
_____ _____
_____ _____
_____ _____

Professional services I regularly use: Potential contacts:

_____ _____
_____ _____
_____ _____
_____ _____

Hobbies/sports interests:

_____

_____

_____

_____

_____

_____

_____

Potential contacts:

_____

_____

_____

_____

_____

_____

_____

I donate time or service on the
following boards of organizations:

_____

_____

_____

_____

_____

_____

Potential contacts:

_____

_____

_____

_____

_____

_____

Organizations I would enjoy
becoming a member of:

_____

_____

_____

_____

_____

_____

Potential contacts:

_____

_____

_____

_____

_____

_____

friend. However, if you are clear about the value of what you offer you are, in fact, verbalizing not a need but an opportunity.

Consider your neighbors who might benefit from what you are offering. Continue by listing potential customers you might meet while commuting, while visiting a restaurant or a department store, and especially during social occasions that lend themselves to idle chatter. List five friends or acquaintances you can call each day to talk about what you are offering. This kind of effort pays off in new business and growing awareness of your operation.

Always carry a business card, a note pad, a brochure, and if possible a sample of what you offer. Becoming a master of public relations simply requires that you remain conscious of who you are and the value of what you offer.

Of course there are those times when you want to separate yourself from business. Understandable. But the main point here is the untapped resources in your life that might yield real benefits if you are willing to be your own publicist.

Personal PR

Another key to attracting customers is a healthy, confident smile. It tells people that what you have is valuable and joyful. A meticulously attired individual who has an appealing manner and is well versed about the product or service being offered is always the most successful salesperson.

People who are successful have an effective personal public relations campaign; they like themselves. They are aware of their own value and are able to explain the quality of their skills in a way that fosters accomplishing their goals.

If you doubt my contention, look around you. Observe your close friends and watch the successful ones practice their public relations. They are the winners—the first to be promoted into higher office positions, the ones who get a date with the special person you've been only eyeing and hoping to attract through some divine miracle.

Your task is to become more proficient at promoting yourself to the people you want to reach and to have them select your personal package. Start by taking a positive personal inventory. (See page 26.) Are you certain about who you are? Have you listed your attributes recently? Have you considered what it is that's special about you as an individual—the unique aspect of your being that sets you apart? What are your endearing qualities?

Having trouble? List the characteristics you find appealing in others. Most likely they are ones you also exhibit. Have confidence. Smile. You're ready to go.

PERSONAL PR INVENTORY

List ten special skills you possess. _____

_____ _____ _____

_____ _____ _____

_____ _____ _____

Of these ten special skills, which three are you absolutely extraordinary at executing? _____ _____ _____

What ten characteristics do you like most in yourself? _____

_____ _____ _____

_____ _____ _____

_____ _____ _____

What is so cute about you that you can't help smiling when you think about it?
_____

What's your favorite asset? _____

Why would you especially want to choose you as a friend?_____

What is most appealing about your disposition?_____

What is most appealing about your appearance?_____

Name three instances in which you have felt especially proud of your accomplishments. _____ _____ _____

If you were giving major awards today, what would be a reason to reward yourself?_____

In what ways does your product or service reflect your special attributes and personality?_____

How can more of what makes you special be made part of your business?_____

_____

The Entrepreneur's Reflection

Your business is an extension of who you are: this is most true of small businesses but also true of larger operations (since big businesses are an extension of the creator who chooses the managers). If the business is unhealthy and unable to attract customers, the owner should see this problem as a reflection of the image being presented. A key to rejuvenating your business is to revitalize yourself and your self-image.

PART
TWO

Creating Your Own
Promotional Campaign

5

Telling Your Story in a Way that Excites the Media

In order to attract the interest of media decision makers you need to acquire the skill of describing products or services in a provocative and newsworthy manner. Editors and producers must be convinced your presentation will not bore their audiences.

All of us, at one time or another, have flipped the television dial, clicked off the radio, or tossed aside the newspaper because we were bored. Now it's your turn on the hot seat! It's your turn to interest viewers, listeners, and readers. It's your turn to keep your audience so enthralled that they don't turn away from what you are saying. When you think you are able to sustain audience interest while describing your product or service, assemble ten honest friends, deliver a presentation, and listen to their response.

Being aware of current topics discussed on the airwaves and in print is an advantage when attempting to gain access to the media. Take note of the kinds of people and products that dominate the specific shows on which you might appear. How does your story compare to what you see and hear? How can you connect your story to current news and provide an unusual perspective? Can you offer something totally different?

One universal topic that provides ongoing focus for the media is the economy: Who has jobs? Who doesn't? Let us suppose that after being laid off from your computer job because of a corporate takeover you retrained and secured a small-business loan to open a bookbinding business. If you were to seek media coverage just for your new business binding rare books, you might find little interest. However, were you to approach media decision makers with the story of your triumph over unemployment you would be much more likely to generate interest. By relating your topic to one of current concern you make your story appealing.

Suppose you are a financial counselor. In order to sell your story to editors and producers, you might decide to donate four hours a week providing telephone counseling for families whose breadwinners are affected by layoffs. This is called using a "story peg"—pegging into what is already of topical interest to audiences. Donating your service to a worthwhile cause or donating proceeds from your business, no matter the size of the amount, could present a reason for media interest in your business.

For example, if you are opening a restaurant you could elect to contribute a portion of your first two nights' receipts to the homeless, to handicapped children, to the blind, or to a local Red Cross chapter. Your donation presents an opportunity for you to write and distribute a media release that subtly notes your contribution. But first inquire whether the organization has provisions for generating publicity. If it does, cooperate with their effort, checking to make certain you are included in the organization's plans.

Even if you are included you may diplomatically tell the staff that you have prepared your own media release. In the best possible situation the writing and distribution should be a joint effort. But the bottom line is that you create an opportunity to invite the media to your restaurant to witness your generous donation.

To stimulate media interest, you might get the mayor or other city officials or any local celebrity to wait tables on that evening. The appearance of any "star" is all the more reason for the media to be fascinated and to print or air a story featuring your restaurant.

A sample media release for such an occasion appears on page 33.

Although associating yourself with what is already news can serve to your advantage, you should have genuine interest in the community project you choose. Insincerity stands out like a siren blasting at midnight.

The recipients of your media release—media outlets—have special requirements for what they see as a workable story. Producers or editors will always analyze your story by asking themselves the following questions: What will most interest the audience? What is suitable for televising? What kinds of visual action can you provide that will demonstrate your point? What in the story will strike the fancy of the listeners? What will rivet the reader to the page? Is there a wonderful anecdote about the way your product is being used that will hold a reader's or listener's interest?

As you begin preparing your materials, explore ways in which your product relates to the safety, financial status, or love life of your audience. Pinpoint an aspect of your story that relates to viewers' ongoing personal interests. How is it that your product or service will improve readers or make them feel better? How can you present your topic that will speak directly to listeners' needs and hold their attention?

NEWS RELEASE
Epicure Delux
17 Parson's Way
Delight, Texas 88799

For Immediate Release

For more information
contact: Guy Winstead
tel: 999-9999

A FEAST FOR THOSE IN FAMINE

Senior shut-ins will feast during the gala opening of the Epicure Delux restaurant on September 1. During the first night of the opening Epicure will provide one hundred free gourmet meals, delivered to senior shut-ins by Meals for Seniors volunteers. Proceeds from one third of the meals sold during the restaurant's opening week will go to feed those who are served by Meals for Seniors.

On September 1, executives and board members of Meals for Seniors, Vice-Mayor Jordan, and other surprise local celebrities will be waiting tables at Epicure to emphasize the need for help in serving meals to shut-ins who would otherwise go hungry.

Says Epicure Delux owner Guy Winstead, "We feel our well-balanced, family-style meals are nutritious and satisfying. We're especially pleased to be able to share fresh, first-rate food with those who can't come in person to enjoy our delightful ambience."

Meals for Seniors board member Brent Jones says, "Getting the gourmet dinners from Epicure will be a special treat for our clients."

MEDIA RELEASE

The biggest question you must answer is that old bugaboo: how are you different from all the others?

Feature or Hard News?

In formulating your approach to the media you must first decide whether you are proposing a feature story or a hard news item. Hard news is an event or issue undergoing urgent development right now, someone or something critical to public safety or survival. It usually is an issue that directly affects the welfare of a large number of people. The following is an example of a lead to a hard news story:

> Seventy-five elderly people are out on the streets this evening. They're being evicted from their homes because members of the state legislature are voting to cut off state funds.

A feature story may examine the human interest side of a straight news story. For example, a feature related to the above news item would be the profile of one of the people being evicted, detailing the hardships she faces in locating another home.

Each day decisions are made about what goes into a newscast based on the news items available that day. If there are two fires, three murders, one robbery, and an election, the weight of the news would be "hard" or "straight." Time and space requirements for the peak events of the day would dictate that most of the "soft" or feature items be relegated to a very few minutes at the end of the newscasts or to talk shows, or, in the case of periodicals, to the lifestyle sections.

Both electronic and print media prefer a balanced picture—one that includes local, national, and international news, along with a pleasant blend of feature items.

On a slow news day, when little is happening, the very soft story—such as a feature about youngsters learning to fly their own kites—could become the highlight of the newscast. (A slight exaggeration, perhaps.)

Observe the flow of the newscasts you watch or the stories you read and you will notice that the format changes from day to day.

Creating an Effective Media Release

A media release—sometimes called a press release or a news release—is your initial method of communicating with editors and producers. It is a one-page document that announces you have valuable information and wish to appear on a news program, talk show, or in the newspaper. Decision makers understand the media release as a request to be seen or heard.

There is a standard formula for writing an effective media release. It should read precisely as you would want to see your story in print, with the facts stated in the order you want the reporter to write them. You need to provide all pertinent descriptions and quotations, just as though *you* were writing the newspaper article.

There is a journalistic formula for creating accurate, interesting, and informative news stories. It is called the inverted pyramid. All stories are based on providing information that answers six questions structured within the inverted pyramid: WHO? WHAT? WHEN? WHERE? HOW? WHY? By adapting the order of these questions to reflect the emphasis of the story, you can be certain of including and presenting all information in the most cohesive and informative manner:

A major rain storm (WHAT)

struck the Oregon coast (WHERE)

making hundreds of residents homeless (WHO)

during last night's (WHEN)

incredible winds that caused tremendous damage (HOW)

because the hurricane's high winds came without warning. (WHY)

Assuming the WHAT of the story is the most important element, it becomes the subject of the first sentence of copy, the lead, which aims to hook the reader's interest and introduce the major journalistic questions. Discussion of the WHAT receives more air time or more print space than any other aspect of the story. As you descend into the story (the inverted pyramid), each sequential question receives less space. This formula makes it simple for a print editor to cut stories from the bottom in accordance with space needs, without deleting vital information.

Now suppose the story were different. Let's say someone significant such as the president of the United States gets caught in a major storm that delays and isolates him on the Oregon coast. The sequence of elements changes:

President Bush (WHO)

was caught in the high winds of a storm (WHAT)

that trapped him on the Oregon coast (WHERE)

yesterday evening as he was en route to... (WHEN)

By rearranging the sequence of these key elements you can shape the nature of the story and ensure clarity, accuracy, and immediacy. The lead element is always the aspect that is most important and most urgent. If a famous person is involved the media release begins with the name of that person in the lead sentence. However, if the person's name is not well known the action or issue of the story becomes the lead.

Using this format will help you structure your media release to tell a story that is both clear and provocative. Pages 36 through 41 illustrate three approaches to the same story.

LEAD: WHAT

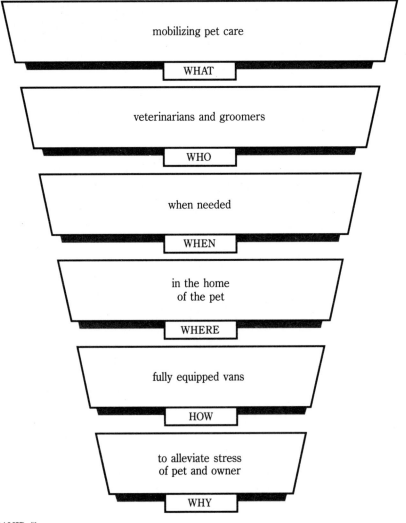

mobilizing pet care

WHAT

veterinarians and groomers

WHO

when needed

WHEN

in the home
of the pet

WHERE

fully equipped vans

HOW

to alleviate stress
of pet and owner

WHY

PYRAMID #1

MOBILIZING PET CARE
Mobilvet Medical and Grooming Service
1111 First Street
First Town, Washington 08532

For Immediate Release

For more information
contact: Wolf Jackson
tel: YOU-RPET

THERE'S NO PLACE LIKE HOME

Creatures large and small find a real discomfort in having to travel across town to a strange environment for medical treatment or grooming. Mobilvet Medical and Grooming Service has solved the problem with its unique fleet of vehicles that go wherever your pet needs care.

Because of today's busy lifestyles pets may suffer from lack of medical attention. For the pet owners, there is often time-consuming stress when chasing the cat or dog and then dragging it into the car for a traumatic trip to the vet or groomer.

There's no doubt that any pet is more comfortable at home. It feels secure and calm; therefore, submitting the animal to the veterinarian's stethoscope or groomer's clippers becomes less traumatic for the owner as well. Mobilvet pet care brings joy and harmony to both owner and pet.

Pet owners say that the mobile service may be more expensive, but it saves them time and money in the long run. Often, when pets require urgent medical care, getting that care on their home turf can prevent hospitalization. "Somehow, being able to retire to a familiar bed is always the best remedy, no matter what the physical complaint," says Mobilvet owner Wolf Jackson.

MEDIA RELEASE

MEDIA RELEASE #1   LEAD: WHAT

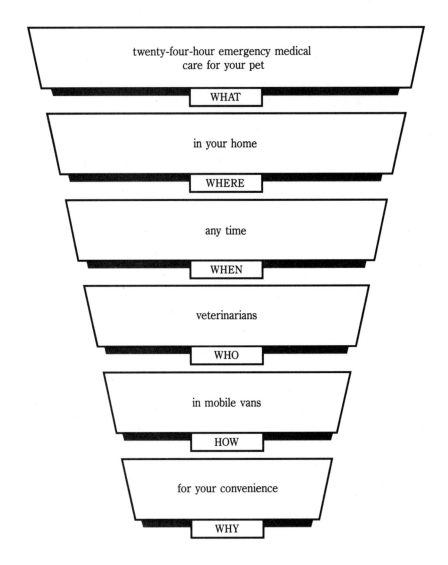

PYRAMID #2

MOBILIZING PET CARE
Mobilvet Medical and Grooming Service
2222 Second Street
Second Town, Washington 08532

For Immediate Release

For more information
contact: Wolf Jackson
tel: YOU-RPET

EMERGENCY PET CARE, WHEN YOU NEED IT!

That midnight whimper of your favorite pet may no longer upset your household. Mobilvet Medical and Grooming Service will immediately respond whenever your pet has an emergency. The unique twenty-four-hour service is believed to be the only one of its kind in this area, and perhaps in the nation.

The practitioners at Mobilvet pride themselves on their quick response to pet owners who call from within a forty-mile radius of Mobilvet's facility. They guarantee customers an emergency response within thirty minutes. Should they fail to do so they will provide free medical care for that occasion. Non-emergency response to ailing pets is scheduled within four hours of the request. The mobile veterinarians also carry a wide range of canine medicines to fill needed prescriptions.

The cost of the Mobilvet emergency medical response service is only 15 to 20 percent higher than the fee of any stationary emergency veterinary service.

Pet owners have the option of purchasing an insurance policy that defrays half the cost of as many as five emergency home calls each year. Mobilvet owner Wolf Jackson says the service is especially valuable for senior citizens or shut-ins who might otherwise not keep pets because of an inability to take them out for grooming or health care.

MEDIA RELEASE

MEDIA RELEASE #2   LEAD: WHAT, ALTERNATIVE

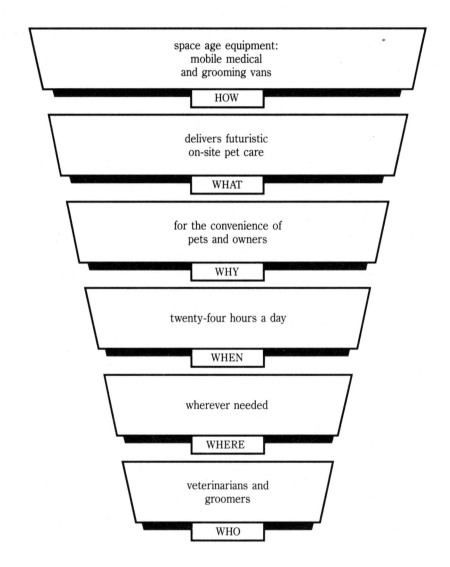

space age equipment:
mobile medical
and grooming vans

HOW

delivers futuristic
on-site pet care

WHAT

for the convenience of
pets and owners

WHY

twenty-four hours a day

WHEN

wherever needed

WHERE

veterinarians and
groomers

WHO

PYRAMID #3

MOBILE MEDICAL AND GROOMING VANS
Mobilvet Medical and Grooming Service
3333 Third Street
Third Town, Washington 08532

For Immediate Release

For more information
contact: Wolf Jackson
tel: YOU-RPET

MOBILVET VANS—A WAY OF THE FUTURE

The sky-blue vans with the Mobilvet sign on the side may look to you like ordinary vehicles driving down the street, but they carry extraordinary equipment that enables veterinarians to respond to the critical emergency needs of ailing or injured pets.

These vans are equipped with state-of-the-art medical instrumentation. Mobilvet owner Wolf Jackson says that the vans have a fully operating mini-medical theater, complete with oxygen tank, x-ray unit, and anesthesiology machine. "We are fully capable of performing medical procedures on animals whose lives might be saved by critically timed surgery."

Mobilvet also has similar vehicles that allow groomers to respond to the call of pet owners who don't have time or energy to do needed pet grooming. Grooming vans are equipped with a shower apparatus that needs only to be hooked up to a hose connection outside your home. Electrical outlets enable the groomer to use the same instruments as in the permanent facility.

"It's always an enjoyable occasion because the pet has remained within its own home," says Jackson.

Mobilvet's fees range from 15 to 20 percent higher than those charged for on-site services. The company was started four years ago and is the only one of its kind, according to Jackson.

MEDIA RELEASE

MEDIA RELEASE #3   LEAD: HOW

Having studied these examples, you are ready to begin formatting your own media release. The pyramid on this page allows you to structure the elements you will use. One way to start is to list significant features of your story. What are the most exciting points? How do they relate to each other? What supporting information builds toward an interesting story that will attract the attention of editors and producers?

Juxtaposing these elements and creating an intriguing scenario will help you structure a media release that attracts the coverage you desire.

LEAD:

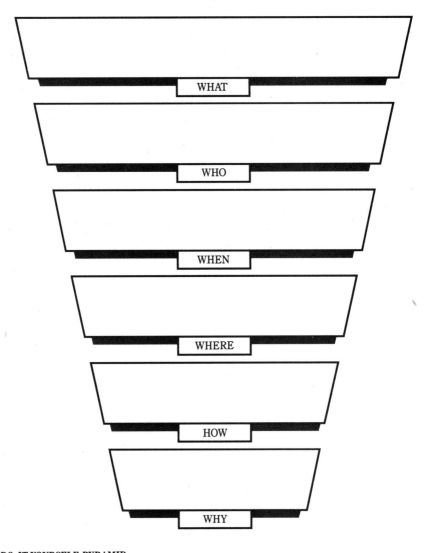

DO-IT-YOURSELF PYRAMID

Polishing Your Media Release

Now that you've organized your information, you need to embellish the steps of the pyramid. Here are the finishing touches for your media release.

FOR IMMEDIATE RELEASE
Usually placed in the upper left corner of the release. On rare occasions you might request a hold on information by giving a date in the future: For release October 18, 1990.

FOR MORE INFORMATION
The name of a responsible, articulate person with facts. Telephone: The number should be one that is not otherwise tied up, so media folks can reach the contact person.

THE HEADLINE OR SUBJECT TITLE
Four to six magnificent, provocative, descriptive words.

THE PARAGRAPHS
Paragraph 1. Begins with summary lead that tells the WHO, WHAT, WHEN, WHERE, HOW, and WHY of your story. The lead must catch and hold the busy reader's attention. It should be provocative, brisk, and urgent in tone. To achieve this effect, use active verbs and short, punchy sentences. You are restating the headline information and supporting your contention that this is a must-cover event.

Paragraph 2. Expands upon the information that supports your lead. It explains why the information is important and what makes it special. Quote your expert spokesperson, organization, or those affected by the action within your story.

Paragraph 3. Give brief background information as further proof of the validity of your event or action. Be accurate about names, dates, and places. Strip from your copy superlatives or padding that would lead an editor or producer to conclude that your media release is solely an effort to get free advertising. A media release is not like an advertisement in which you can be blatant about promoting yourself or your product. Glitzy words describing the extravagant, earth-shaking nature of your event or action just won't be believed. Editors want "just the facts."

Paragraph 4. This is the time to give details showing that what you are doing will appeal to the viewing/listening/reading audience. How will it affect them? Who would otherwise suffer, be unemployed, face dire consequences, or be evicted? Who will benefit from the toxic waste cleanup or from lowered insurance rates?

Keep in mind that the information should be factual and presented as dramatically as possible. Although your aim above all else is to emphasize the news value of your story, do not exaggerate. There is no excuse for misleading members of the media. Their credibility can be jeopardized by your not telling the truth. If you lie or overdramatize you risk forfeiting your access to coverage.

Paragraph 5. If there is space available, use additional paragraphs to indicate what action might be taken by the public in response to your story. For example: "Send telegrams to Senator Dawson to stop the wasting of water in the state park," or "Volunteers interested in helping the seniors' food garden may call 999-9999 or come to 12 Maple Avenue."

Paragraph 6. Admission prices, RSVP information, and other details not previously included should go next. You might want to mention another event to be held in conjunction with the one covered by your lead.

Final paragraph. Ending paragraphs are the place for information that is of least importance to your story, since an editor will usually start cutting verbiage from the bottom. The last line might provide additional opportunities for coverage: your spokesperson is in town and is available for interviews, the author will be signing books at Hinkley's on Tuesday, or she will be speaking at the Woman's Club on next Thursday. (Be aware, however, that giving members of the media options of where to interview the star of your news conference could work against your goal. They might elect to interview your star at those places, thereby killing the lead of your story.)

The resulting media release should be short, brisk, and effective. (See release on page 33.)

Media-Release Writer's Block

Stark raving terror! Fear! The word *write* sometimes creates panic in the hearts of even the most competent and successful businesspeople.

If you can't get past this barrier and write your own media release, hire a professional promotional copywriter. You can't afford to get stuck in fear and let the bogeyman spoil your success in promoting yourself.

You will want copywriters to answer these questions before hiring one: What have they done before? Can they give you someone to call for a reference? What is their fee per hour? How long will it take them to write your media release? Get an agreement in writing and move ahead.

If, on the other hand, you have written a media release but are unhappy or unsure about its form and content, look for an editor. Most communities have media workshops and referral services. Some television and radio stations have public service offices staffed with smiling people eager to help you gain access to their station's free time. Ask and you will find the assistance you need. Let nothing deter your efforts to exercise your PR power.

For Immediate Release

For more information
contact: Ms. Promotion
tel: (415) 000-0000

PR POWER BOOSTS SMALL-BUSINESS SALES

Small-business owners across the country report increased income due to exercising what they are calling their Public Relations Power. The catalyst for this enthusiasm is the book *Expose Yourself* by businesswoman Melba Beals, which guides business owners to promote themselves for profit and fun.

By learning the skills necessary to conduct public relations campaigns, entrepreneurs are using the media to reach large numbers of buyers. *Expose Yourself* is generating increased sales and earnings.

Small Business Owners Association head John Q. Smythe says, "Entrepreneurs are learning how to take advantage of the millions of dollars in free advertising available on the air and in print." Smythe says a staggeringly large number of small-business firms are forced to close their doors each year. "Most of these failures are due to lack of sales because the owners of the firms don't know how to promote themselves," he reports.

Says Smythe, "As their numbers increase, it will be even more crucial for small-business owners to learn public relations skills in order to survive."

Based on her twenty years experience working for both the electronic and print media, Beals has devised a formula for strategizing public relations campaigns that increase sales and build a favorable public image.

"Many business owners are losing opportunities for creating sales because they believe publicity campaigns are for big corporations or 'other' companies," says Beals. "But inside every business is a great story. With my book as their guide, entrepreneurs will easily be able to identify that story and position it with the media so that it reaches an appreciative public."

The step-by-step guide is published by the San Francisco–based Chronicle Books. Affordably priced at $18.95, the book is available in bookstores everywhere.

MEDIA RELEASE

Non-Event Media Releases

In addition to calling attention to specific, timely events, media releases can be used for "non-events," when you have some ongoing issue that might be of interest to the public. Examples of such situations might be announcing a unique kind of medical clinic staffed only by women and offering women's health care from a feminine perspective; a change in direction for an already announced event; or a change in the focus of your business, such as a scavenger company initiating a plan for ridding the environment of toxic waste.

On these occasions you may elect to use the same form for the media releases shown previously, but you would mail it only to feature desks or the news outlets specifically appropriate to your story. In other words, you would not treat it as hard news.

Non-event releases differ only in that they emphasize the human interest aspect or a change in the status quo. These documents might be a bit more chatty. Since their focus is different they may not fit exactly into the hard news format, but that is no reason to abandon the basic principles of a media release.

Media-Release Checklist

- Keep your release brisk and short, approximately 250 words, double spaced. Keep it to one page. If an earth-shaking event demands that you take more than one page of copy, also put the name, title, and phone number of your contact person at the top of the second page. Do not divide paragraphs between pages.
- Use only one side of the page.
- Obey the standard edicts for proper margins—at least one inch on each side and at the top and bottom.
- All materials should include your name, address, and telephone number in the upper-right-hand corner.
- Name a spokesperson at the top right of the release: *For more information contact Ms. Spokesperson.* Your spokesperson must be able to explain all the data included in your media release.
- Edit your material, taking out extrinsic information and soft details.
- Tell your story with feeling, color, and flair. Ordinary is not interesting.
- Tell your story in the way you hope it will be aired or printed.
- Don't hype yourself or your story. Editors want the facts, not an advertisement.
- Be ready to point out the human-interest side of your story. Who will be affected? How does what you offer touch lives? In what way can every listener or reader feel empathy for your point of view?

- Check and double check names, dates, places, and times. Your goal is to achieve 100 percent accuracy.
- Provide verifiable information. Don't make wild unsubstantiated claims you can't support. Don't include secondhand information.
- Use correct grammar and proper syntax.
- Choose paper in a color that is in concert with the tone of your event or action and that reflects the image of your business or organization. Use a format that looks crisp, neat, and professional.
- Take a last look at the preliminary copy of your release. Is this information easy for the editor to understand? Has the release been written with the interests of the media audience in mind? Will it further your objectives in exposure for your service or product?

The sample media releases shown throughout this book use one of many possible layouts; your releases can be on your letterhead stationery or on blank paper, and you can vary the placement of the company name and address, contact person, and the words "media release" or "news release." It is most important that the message be clear: the form of the release should not obscure its basic purpose—to convey information.

Creating an effective media release will enable you to tell your story in a way that excites the media and yields maximum exposure.

6

Using the Media Packet
as Your Messenger

Sending a media packet, or kit, can often be a real boost to your efforts to get publicity. It is a convenient messenger that can tell the media assignment editor who you are and what you offer. It is your opportunity to go beyond a media release and create a concise and attractive package of information that represents your point of view and can indeed improve your chances for placement—for getting into the newspaper or on the TV show.

Conversely, an unprofessional media packet, or one lacking relevant thematic information, can work to your detriment. Be certain that your packet presents you in a way that will enhance your image and opportunity.

When you provide editors and producers with attractive media kits, you familiarize them with the quality of your work and your skills at presentation. If you present cogent information in print and communicate with flair, you assure them that you will be able to communicate with their audience in a satisfactory manner. Including your photograph will ease the decision makers' minds by letting them know you are neither Attila the Hun nor Godzilla. The more you reveal in your packet about the credibility of your information, the appropriateness of your presentation, and the appeal of your public persona, the more you assure producers and editors that presenting you and your story will be pleasing to their audiences. They wish to avoid any possibility of disaster, and they want to sell newspapers and get high ratings.

In addition, producers and editors are always harried by intense time pressures, so they appreciate thorough digests of information about your special product, issue, or service that precludes their needing to research facts or devise focus points. You can assist this process by including a list of points that might interest the audience. You do the editors and yourself a favor by making it easier for them to present your topic.

Of course one major consideration in making the decision to invest in a media packet is the cost. Compare the cost of mailing a single sheet of paper in a #10 envelope (standard business size) requiring standard postage with the cost of mailing a ten-by-twelve-inch manila envelope containing your media kit. The extra postage can be five to ten times the cost of mailing a single sheet. Add to that the cost of supplies, copies, photography, and printing as well as the time required to assemble a kit, and you run up quite a tab in money and energy.

On the basis of budget you may decide not to compile a media packet at this point in your promotional campaign. Don't let that decision deter you from moving full steam ahead with your self-promotion. Yes, a media packet is a wonderful tool. But the fact is you can also gain access to the media with a well-written, single-page release. After assessing your current resources of time, energy, and money, decide on the campaign strategy that best suits your need.

Assembling a Media Kit

A double-pocket portfolio gives you the opportunity to include your media release, event schedule, fact sheet, photograph, any previously published articles about your endeavors, biography, and briefing or background sheet. If, for example, you are planning a grand opening celebration for your grocery shopping service, your packet might include the following single sheets:

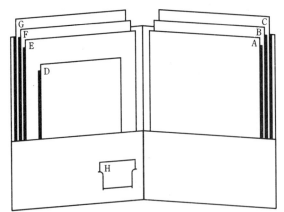

A. Media release	E. Articles previously published on you or your business
B. Event schedule	F. Biography
C. Fact sheet	G. Briefing or background information
D. Photograph	H. Business card or other identification

A. *Media release:* This single sheet announces the event. As described in Chapter Five, it begins with a strong lead that will catch the attention of the editor or producer. It then gives an overview of your service, the event, and its special significance to the public.

B. *Event schedule:* If you're handling a complex event with many different activities occurring over a period of time, send a schedule on a separate page. Media representatives, and especially electronic media crews, are conscious of time deadlines. They appreciate notes warning them of special circumstances. For example:

Mayor due to cut ribbon at 3:05 p.m.
(In-and-out appearance. On wheels at 3:13 p.m.)

[This parenthetical note signals reporters they have only about ten minutes available to cover the mayor.]
Caution: this kind of information must be accurate. If there are last-minute changes, telephone your media contact.

C. *Fact sheet:* This explains in more detail the significant points of your service. Highlight the aspects that set you apart from other, similar services. You might want to note that you buy from local farmers who provide fresh produce each day.

D. *Photograph:* Use an eight-by-ten-inch glossy black-and-white photo that shows you delivering groceries, behind the counter with lots of customers milling about, or in another work-related situation. Choose a professional photographer; your publicity photo could be used by some newspapers as a part of their story on your business. Even though you might be tempted, avoid at all cost having Uncle Ted or Aunt Lucy or your son take the picture. Only if it's professional looking and in focus is a picture worth a thousand words.

E. *Previous articles:* Include one or two recent articles written about you and/or your business in recognized newspapers or magazines. The information should be relevant to your current endeavor. Avoid sending clippings from your church bulletin or country club newsletter. Caution: a surefire way to turn off reporters is to send them a very recent article featuring your story written by a competitor. Take care not to submit articles to competing newspapers. If the article from the competing paper is a year old and there have been significant changes in what you do, then perhaps you might include it.

F. *Biography:* Even the most compelling urge to begin with "I was born in..." and to fill in your life's events to the present should be resisted. Details about yourself, your ancestors, and your pet duck should be mentioned only as they relate to the grocery service and your opening. The bio should be a briskly written one-page document that weaves facts about your education and background into a scenario centered on your current business. Were you a champion roller skater? If you plan to deliver groceries on roller skates, then—and only then—that piece of information may become a part of your bio.

G. *Briefing or background sheet:* Use this sheet to explain the history of the development of shopping services in general and yours in particular. Note: This information may be combined with your biography and under certain circumstances could provide the core material for the bio.

Include each document only when it serves a specific purpose. If your media contact person gets bogged down by a profusion of irrelevant facts in an overdone packet, he or she won't have the time or the inclination to determine whether you're a good prospect for a talk show or feature story.

Going All Out for Packaging

The appropriate media packet can attract favorable attention and give you a little edge that boosts you into an available spot on the airwaves or in the newspaper. When you are vying for such a chosen spot it is best to take time to decide about just the kind of packaging that will best represent you and your business.

Will you opt for a color-coordinated packet printed on slick stock (Krome Kote paper), with your logo embossed on the outside cover? Or, in keeping with a shoestring budget, will you choose portfolios and color-coordinated paper sold at a reasonable price in your local stationery store? Within the limits of a modest budget, you can use your creative flair to compile a professional media packet.

Another option is the use of clever alternative packaging. The owner of a restaurant specializing in take-out food chose to deliver his media releases and bio in specially designed brown paper bags. One business had press materials delivered in white gift boxes with fancy ribbons. As an even larger project, a gourmet baker had berry pies delivered, simultaneously, to media outlets throughout the city. The pies were sent atop cardboard containers that housed media materials announcing the opening of his new bakery.

I have witnessed any number of clever and too-clever press gimmicks at the desks of assignment editors. Some were hits. Others were complete misses; that is, they were the kinds of flops that generated a raising of editors' eyebrows and perhaps a snicker or two before they were tossed into the trash. Careful! To execute a catchy campaign, particularly a large one, you need savvy, time, money, energy, and a willingness to regroup should your initial approach not succeed.

The most cleverly designed package in the world will not be welcome if it falls apart when it is handled or if it forces the editor to take time out from a hectic schedule to wash sticky desktops. You don't want to add clutter to an editor's life. Your goal is to send your media materials in a format that is seductive, alluring, and informational, in a form that is functional and easy to handle.

What Hidden Messages Are You Sending?

Be aware that the color, layout, and design of your media packet send a message that is often far more revealing than even your written words. Sometimes that message is contrary to the image you wish to convey. (Remember the discussion in Chapter Three about painting an appropriate self-portrait.)

If you are a nonprofit organization urging the media and the public to support your fund-raiser but your media kit is outrageously slick, the message is that you already have enough extra money to spend. If you are a fashion consultant but you send media packets in dreary colors, the message is that you are unimaginative in the way you dress your clients.

Suppose you are a physical fitness expert who claims to have developed an exercise program that will make the whole of Western civilization thin and fit. Your photography, however, shows you and your staff members with tummies hanging over your belts. You have failed to give evidence that supports the contention in your materials.

Keep in mind that what you mail to the media acts as your representative, conveying covert as well as overt messages about who you are. Based on their initial impression of your media packet, producers and editors will decide whether your request for space or time should receive serious consideration.

7

Locating, Building, and Using Media Lists

A critical tool for any successful public relations campaign is the media list. It is the key to an effective mailing and follow-up, and can literally make the difference between the roaring success or dismal failure of your promotional efforts. After all, even the world's best media kit can do no good unless it gets into the hands of the right people.

A professional publicist spends endless hours tailoring a proper media list to serve each client's specific needs. Having a meticulously updated list or knowing where to locate one is a major component in the package the publicist sells to a client. Only in very rare circumstances would a publicist lend or sell a personalized media list. As one working publicist says, "Ask to borrow my husband of ten years and you're likely to get a civil response. Ask for my media list and I pull my sword."

Since you probably don't want to expend the long hours to do all the research yourself, the core of your media list will come from a media directory. *You must constantly update your list with current media contact names and job titles.* Within the broadcast and print media personnel turnover is swift. "Here today, gone tomorrow" is putting it mildly. More likely it's "here this morning, gone this afternoon." Therefore any media directory you acquire will be out of date even as you hand your money across the counter to pay for it. Many directories send buyers frequent update sheets. Still, there is no way to avoid putting some time and energy into updating.

It is rare to find a single media directory that supplies the one list especially suited to your particular promotional requirements. Rather, the most efficient working list usually comes from a compilation of the materials in several directories and then a personal selection process.

How to Use Media Directories

Media directories organize information in various ways: by type of media, by size of audience, by geographic area, by subject matter, and by a combination of these categories.

One category might be women's magazines and another might be newsletters of organizations. Another directory might specify the top one hundred radio stations for rock music and have a separate category for the top one hundred markets in the nation. "Top" means rated highest according to the size of audience. For each top market, the directory would list all the media outlets in the geographic area—New York City or the San Francisco Bay Area, for example. Several national directories list daily and weekly newspapers, general circulation magazines, commercial television stations, and radio stations.

If you are planning a national mailing, you might choose to mail to all the media within the top fifty markets, including newspapers, radio stations, and television stations. Another choice might be to mail only to specialty magazines—entertainment, environment, gay, finance, home business owners, farm and ranch, seniors, ethnic, or religious—depending on the nature of your business. Chances are, if there is a media outlet you can specifically define, someone has already compiled a list of names to match your need.

If your promotional campaign calls for local media marketing, you could choose all media within a geographic area, or just local media with a specific focus, such as newspapers with special interests, radio talk-show programs, or organizational newsletters within an industry.

These are just a few of the numerous categories of lists available to you. By using a combination of directories you can develop your own comprehensive, individualized list. An adequately compiled directory will list and cross-reference media outlets, addresses, call letters of broadcast outlets, telephone numbers, brief descriptions of content and focus, types of guests or information requested, and the name of the contact people.

Radio and television directories should list names of news producers as well as talk-show and community-affairs contacts. Some directories will give additional information on audience size, typical age range, and interests. For magazines, directories will report circulation, how frequently topics are covered in specific sections, and which editor is responsible for compiling each of those sections. Some directories reveal whether or not the periodical accepts media releases or new product ideas.

Locating Media Directories

For an economical source of media data, try local libraries and chambers of commerce in your area. Most will have adequate media reference material. You might also check your local telephone directory and jot down some basic names and phone numbers.

Nonprofit groups and community colleges across the country offer directories and often can provide you with current media lists and knowledgeable advisors.

You may want to order creditable national media directories by mail. It is a worthwhile investment, especially if you intend to mount a public relations campaign for products or services that have national interest. To defray expenses, you can form a resource bank with fellow business owners. Newcomers are well advised to begin by using library and chamber resources until they can ascertain which of the directories best suits their needs. Directories can be very costly.

A list of some useful directories and their approximate prices follows.

Advertising & Publicity Resources for
Scholarly Books
Association of American University Presses
584 Broadway, Suite 410
New York, NY 10012
(212) 941-6610
Price: $200

Information on some 3,200 periodicals in 45 categories.

All in One Directory
Gebbie Press, Inc.
P.O. Box 1000
New Paltz, NY 12561
(914) 255-7560
Price: $73

A consummate guide: newspapers, radio, and TV as well as consumer magazines, professional business publications, trade magazines, farm publications, the black press, and news syndicates.

Bacon's Publicity Checker
Bacon's Publishing Company
332 S. Michigan Avenue
Chicago, IL 60604
(800) 621-0561
Price: $170

Newspapers and magazines, both trade and consumer, television and radio stations. Two volumes.

B.P.I. Media Services
P.O. Box 2015
Lakewood, NJ 08701
(201) 363-5633
Price: $263

Directory of radio contacts in some 300 markets.

Broadcasting/Cablecasting Yearbook
Broadcasting Publications, Inc.
1705 DeSales Street, NW
Washington, DC 20036
(202) 659-2340
Price: $95

Electronic broadcast media: radio (AM and FM), TV, and cable outlets. Includes a history of broadcasting and FCC regulations.

Editor & Publisher International Yearbook
11 W. 19th Street
New York, NY 10011
(212) 675-4380
Price: $70

Daily and Sunday newspapers in the US and Canada, foreign and special service newspapers, black newspapers, clipping bureaus, and house organs.

Hudson's Washington News
Media Contact Directory
P.O. Box 311
Rhinebeck, NY 12572
(914) 876-2081
Price: $119

The Washington press corps: more than 4,000 correspondents.

Media News Keys
40-29 27th Street
Long Island City, NY 11101
(718) 937-3990
Price: $100

Weekly, four-page update showing media personnel information for radio, TV, magazines in the 40 top markets.

The Newsletter Clearinghouse
P.O. Box 311
Rhinebeck, NY 12572
(914) 876-2081
Price: $99

Subscription newsletters by subject and category. Each notation coded to reflect whether publication accepts media releases.

Radio Publicity Outlets
Resource Media, Inc.
P.O. Box 307
Kent, CT 06757
(800) 441-3839
Price: $179

Approximately 3,500 network-syndicated and local talk shows in the nation's 200 major markets; 4,500 local and college radio stations.

Television Factbook
Warren Publishing, Inc.
2115 Ward Court, NW
Washington, DC 20037
(202) 872-9200
Price: $325

Commercial and noncommercial TV stations and networks worldwide.

T.V. Publicity Outlets
Resource Media, Inc.
P.O. Box 307
Kent, CT 06757
(800) 441-3839
Price: $179 per year

Lists 4,000 programs broadcast by TV stations, carried by cable, or distributed by networks or syndicates.

Working Press of the Nation
National Research Bureau
310 S. Michigan Avenue, Suite 1150
Chicago, IL 60604
(312) 663-5580
Price: $290 for complete set
       $135 per volume

Five volumes, one each for newspapers, magazines, radio and TV, free-lance writers and photographers, and corporate publications. Personnel listings, deadlines, and useful sub-categories.

Labels and Mailing Services

Some media directories offer their lists on mailing labels. For an average cost of twenty-five to thirty-five cents per name, depending on how specific the list is and how many names you require, the company will send you labels ready to mail. This is not a purchase but a rental for one-time use only. If you try to copy and reuse the list, the least penalty you risk is never again being able to partake of the service.

Several directories have labeling services that will both target the appropriate market and mail your media release for you. One such company is Bacon's Publicity Checker, 332 S. Michigan Avenue, Chicago, Illinois 60604; (800) 621-0561.

Another organization that offers full-service mailing is the National Press Club, 14th and F Streets, NW, Washington, DC 20045; (202) 737-4434. Other companies that do not publish directories also offer list rentals with complete mailing services. These companies offer services that include printing, stuffing envelopes, reproducing photographs, affixing labels and postage, and completely executing your media mailing for you. One such company is MDS/PRA Group (formerly PR AIDS), 307 W. 36th St., New York, NY 10018; (212) 279-4800.

Suppose you want a special audience—not just members of the news media—to attend an event you are planning. Perhaps you are an acupuncturist: you want a list of all people who are potential clients to attend your demonstration. You could also rent a "target" mailing list, such as of people who subscribe to an acupuncturist magazine in your area. Your source for subscription lists, membership lists, and virtually every other kind of mailing list is a list broker.

List brokers can provide labels that allow you to mail information to absolutely any group you choose. Fish-tank keepers, stamp collectors, underwater basket weavers—whoever you want to attend your event. Check your telephone directory for the list broker of your choice. List brokers and other list services can provide you with very narrowly defined target groups, focusing on the special interest you desire in your project. With a list of subscribers to a scuba-diving magazine, for example, you can specify subcategories: by income, political party, age, sex, religion, number of cars owned, credit cards, number of children, and so on. Some lists pinpoint the target audience by analyzing what charities they have contributed to on previous occasions.

If you rent labels for a local mailing, be careful to select only ZIP codes close to the event you wish attended. Don't expect a news photographer or member of the public to travel two hours to attend your special event unless it is really super special.

A list rental from a broker is not expensive; standard lists range from

$50 to $100 per one thousand names, with an additional charge (about $5) for each subcategory you select (California only, women only, and so on). Labels can be provided four across, on plain paper—called cheshire labels—for affixing by a special machine at a mailing house; self-adhering labels with peel-off backing are often called pressure-sensitive labels.

If you don't want to mail the materials yourself, you can usually find a mailing house in your area. Unlike complete mailing companies that also rent mailing lists and print materials, most mailing houses take the list, envelopes, and printed information you give them and fold, stuff, meter, and sort them, then deliver them to the Post Office.

Before you choose which mailing house and list broker you will use, research those in your area so you avoid wasting time and money. A dishonest broker can saddle you with an outdated list, crammed with names of people who have moved; an inefficient mailing house can delay or mix up your mailing.

Compiling Your List

Choosing the editors or producers you will approach is much easier when you understand their roles and how you can relate your story to their needs. Each magazine, each radio show, each newspaper has a specific format. It is important for you to know that format and the kinds of stories and issues currently being featured.

Take an excursion to your local library. Relax. Allow enough time to explore the periodicals that attract your attention. Examine as many as possible that you think might run a story like your own. Become familiar with their different areas of focus. Is there a section within that periodical that seems especially relevant to your particular story? What writers in your local newspaper appeal to you? Has there ever been a story similar to the one you offer?

Watch the television interview and talk shows, even if you must video-tape shows that air while you are working. Are there slots being aired that lead you to believe your subject is appropriate? What about your favorite radio programs? Would you tune in to hear your topic?

Become aware of media outlets and shows beyond your usual range of interest that might be appropriate for your story. Don't narrow your selections to the periodicals you usually read or the television and radio you always choose.

After jotting down your personalized list and obtaining core list directories, determine whether your particular directories give personal profiles of some of the reporters at your local newspapers or broadcast stations. Many directories tell you precisely what an editor or reporter is looking for. Alternatively, by reading or watching the media, you can get an idea of what subject a reporter usually covers. A sportswriter is probably not going to be interested in new fashion designs. Reporters, editors, and producers are most open to stories that fall somewhat within the range of their interests and the focus of their work.

In locating the appropriate media contact, these are some of the questions you may have to answer: What locally produced shows, other than the news shows, accept guests? To whom should you address your media releases? Who are the news producers for morning, noon, evening, and weekend shows? Is there a special story editor who chooses topics?

With periodicals you will need to answer some or all of these questions: Who is the reporter with special interest in the area you desire? Who is the general assignment editor? Who edits the Sunday magazine? To whom should you address media releases? What are the lead times? (The lead time is how far in advance they require material to be submitted.)

You can always call the station, newspaper, or magazine to check names, but make sure you ask brief, concise questions. And be prepared for harried switchboard operators to connect you with an editor instead of answering your question or spelling the name.

For those whose budgets will not allow the purchase of an almost always expensive directory or of a mailing list, there are several other ways of compiling a workable list. Simply make a list of your favorite media, add names and addresses from the telephone book, and update these by checking magazine and newspaper mastheads and credit "crawls" following the news or other shows that accept guests. The process does not have to be complex or expensive.

Through all of your list making, don't forget specialty periodicals like corporate house organs, organizational newsletters, craft and hobby journals, and airline magazines. These periodicals, read by thousands, are a wonderful resource and often are open to accepting new stories.

Wire Services and Syndicates

Be sure to add appropriate wire services and syndicates to your media lists. These services supply the media with material from local, state, national, and foreign sources by using electronic high-speed systems—wires in the old days, now satellites as well—throughout the country and the world.

In addition to news services such as Associated Press or Reuters, there are specialized wires for insurance, business, entertainment, and other industries. Check your local directory under news wire services. Most of these services provide a daily calendar of events to aid assignment editors in making choices about news coverage.

Another way to gain access to a wire is by renting time from a service. One such company, PR News-Wire, was created in New York City in 1954 and has become a worldwide distribution system.

Syndicates are another important vehicle for reaching many newspapers with a single press release. There are two ways to approach syndicates: with a "spot" feature that the syndicate can offer to its clients, and with a media kit aimed at a syndicated columnist who will mention or review your service or product.

A chapter from your book, twenty-five dry-cleaning hints used in your dry-cleaning business, or health hints from your clinic are all examples of one-shot features that a syndicate could offer. The chances of seeing print through a syndicate are better, however, if you approach an established columnist who writes on a topic related to your product. The annual *Editor & Publisher Syndicate Directory* lists syndicates with addresses and editorial staff; columnists by subject matter; and names of features. A mention in a column has proven very helpful to many businesses.

These wires and syndicates provide an invaluable link to radio, television, and newspapers. They are a way of announcing your story to all media outlets simultaneously and immediately. If you had a legitimate news story and time to make only one phone call, it should be to the wire services, who would (if they selected your story to run), in effect, announce it to everyone.

Maintaining and Updating Your Lists

Compile your lists carefully. Devise a format that allows for current and future notations, including helpful notes about whose daughter is graduating, who is having a baby, who is married to whom, and who is divorcing. Certainly this ought to include decision makers' special hobbies or likes and dislikes when that information is available. Of course, editors' story preferences should be noted. Your system should allow you to reorder, manipulate, and alter lists as you go along.

Some people prefer keeping lists in a loose-leaf binder that can be sectioned according to specific categories. Others use index cards or a large alphabetical Rolodex. Many people use computerized lists, which are a wonderful innovation but not always easy to work with when you are sitting with one ear to the phone or when you are separated from your computer.

Additions to your core list—the list you derived from directories, mailing lists, and telephone books—should include media sources that have special appeal to you. Think about sending your story to a columnist you've read and loved for years, or to the drive-time radio personality show you tune in each morning.

Of course, you will also want to call on any personal contacts you have within the media. Even though their specific area may be inappropriate for your story, ask them who might be interested. The media make an incestuous profession; everybody knows everybody else. A referral from one friend to another can be a tremendous asset for you in persuading someone of the value of your story.

Keep the faith. You will begin your list with what appears to be a hodgepodge of names, call letters, and references. Don't be overwhelmed. It is exciting to assume that you can be chosen to appear on every talk show on your list or be interviewed in each of the periodicals. Next you'll need to harness your excitement and assess realistically your needs and the needs of the media outlets you will approach.

Refine your specialized list by identifying the outlets most appropriate for placement of your story. Is it hard news or soft feature? Are you able to plug your story into what is going on in the news today? What are the varying angles on your story, the diverse points of view that might make it appealing to several different kinds of editors?

It is usually a good idea to send your media release to the news editors (assignment desks) of newspapers and of television and radio stations in your area. If they can't use it they may pass it on, but you run the risk that your materials may end up in the trash. Of course, the best way to ensure initial attention is by sending your release both to a reporter who might have a special interest in your story and to the assignment or news editor.

Targeting the Right Editors and Producers

Using the customer profiles you developed in Chapter Four and the media lists you have compiled, build a profile of the television and radio shows, newspapers, and magazines most likely to reach your target customers. In which audiences are your potential customers likely to be listening and reading? If you are selling products or services that appeal to young mothers, avoid sending media releases to the evening sportscast. If you are selling golf lessons, skip the talk shows that focus on parenting in the 1990s.

In other words, your media audience must match the consumers of your product or service. Use the radio, television, and periodical outlets that act as direct conduits to your potential customers. Consider the gender, age, education, and economic status of the audience; often media directories or mailing list brokers will have these and other demographics. If you are talking about seminars on financial planning, it would not serve your purpose to appear on a radio talk show on a station that caters to teen-oriented music. Instead, direct your energy toward getting a slot on a drive-time commute radio talk show, to which people in the business community are more likely to be listening. Choose a news-talk or call-in show or an all-news station within the morning news format. And remember that most working people are not home for the midday news.

Also, clarify your market area. If your widget is only sold in Oshkosh you'd waste time seeking a slot on a national morning talk show. At the very most, make such a quest very low on your list of priorities unless your widget is extraordinary in nature and will soon be sold across the country or by mail order. What's the point of airing intriguing conversations about something that is not available for purchase? You would only frustrate an audience.

Producers and editors are not usually interested in having you present a product or service that will not be available in their area until next year. What you offer should be immediately available to your audience.

Presenting the right story for the wrong audience or at the wrong time will not bring the results you desire. Understanding and researching the appropriate media outlets for your story will ensure maximum return on your energy investment.

Considering the Needs of the Media

In choosing appropriate media outlets, consider the needs of those producers and editors you will approach. If you were the decision maker, what would be your response to the media packet? In what way does the story you offer enhance the theme of the show? How does the story fit into the format? By what special element will it intrigue and inform the audience?

Be creative in thinking about the ways in which you might adjust your approach to make it more seductive. Suppose you are the one giving golf lessons. What about offering golf as an early morning exercise for young mothers, one that trims the waistline, provides challenge, and quiets the nervous system once the children are off to school? With that approach in mind, golf aligns with parenting after all; make an effort to fill a slot on one of the early morning talk shows for housewives.

You might get a television news editor to do an on-location shot at your place of business if, for example, you can convince decision makers that your financial planning seminars provide moments of exciting visual impact on their audience. Money is universally a good topic for riveting the attention of an audience. However, never assume that your standing before an audience will be enough. *Visuals* are the key to success in television: bring interesting images and action to your presentation.

List ways in which your topic could be appreciated by varying groups of people of all ages, incomes, and backgrounds. This will allow you to begin seeing your topic as the media decision makers see it. Unless you are able to pitch your story on several different levels and tailor it to varying needs, you will be limited in the media coverage you receive.

When to Mail Your Media Release

Timing is an important element in securing media coverage: when and how you mail your media releases can determine the amount and nature of the coverage you will receive. Keep in mind that decision makers should receive your materials well ahead of any scheduled event or action. Mail releases announcing a specific event at least fifteen days ahead of time. Preferably, send an advisory release twenty-five days ahead and mail the full release packet fifteen days in advance.

A media advisory reads like an invitation, stating the nature of the event, date, time, location, and contact person. Depending on the circumstances, you may want to drop in three provocative lines that whet the appetites of the recipients of your notice.

For talk shows and community-service shows, assume at least a six-week lead time. These are general guidelines. Check for the specific schedules that apply to shows in your area. You may live in an isolated community where the media, even with just two to five days' notice, will shout for joy at your request for an appearance. If you live in a large city where media news and talk segments are booked as much as six months ahead, you need to know that. One simple telephone call to the producer will provide the information. Some media guide directories give lead times, but double check their accuracy before relying on them.

Even when a show has a lead time so long it extends beyond your event, send your media release and do your follow-up calling. You never know when you might be just perfect to fill a spot left vacant by a sudden cancellation.

As for newspapers, the fifteen-day rule applies. Magazines have varying lead times—from one week up to nine months. Be aware of what is required.

As mentioned earlier, be certain that your product or service is available when you promote it. An abundant gush of publicity with no product equals no sale. If there is the slightest doubt in your mind about being able to service the requests generated, don't mail your release. Halt! You're wasting your time. You'll anger the public and annoy those media who extended a courtesy by choosing you for exposure.

Also consider that you cannot distribute media releases every other week. In fact, don't mount a major campaign on the same topic more often than once a year. Yes, of course you can find varied "hooks" (story angles) to promote the same product or service, but the point is that you should not mail too often or no one will take you seriously.

When planning a media release distribution, analyze your promotional picture over at least a year. Is there something happening next month or the month after that is a more appropriate focus for your campaign? Would yet another of your products, available early next year, receive a better response?

Is the event you're publicizing the best you will create within the year? If it is not your personal best, then wait for best. Second best does not attract media attention. In fact, second best could so antagonize the media that they would not be interested in responding when you are delivering the ultimate caper. Be aware also of the season of the year—of holidays and the kinds of trends and events that surround them. All these factors play a vital part in whether to schedule your mailing now or later.

Heading for the Mailbox

Having thoroughly analyzed your promotional picture and assembled the list of your most likely prospects, you are ready to mail your media packets. If you are sending requests to talk shows, write a brief cover letter introducing the topic. Brief means two paragraphs at most.

The letter should begin with a two-line introduction to your topic and yourself. Note your credentials for discussing the chosen topic and describe what you are featuring: "See attached materials on the electronic window washer that cleans windows while you sleep," or "I have the secret to making money grow on trees, or at least those who attend my financial seminars describe my method that way."

The brief description of what you are offering must be provocative. Boring descriptions will eliminate any possibility of your being considered.

Following this introduction, state whether you have appeared on other talk shows. Mention that you have been successful at pleasing some audience in the past and refer to specific instances: "I recently spoke before the Chamber of Commerce."

And remember—it is always wise to address media packets to a specific person. When you are approaching a show, get the name of the producer or other contact person. If your event or issue takes place on the weekend, use the name of the weekend assignment editor. Later, as you are involved in follow-up calling, you will be much more efficient if you are able to ask for a specific person by name.

Finally, if you have compiled the packets yourself, double check to see that the materials are assembled in the desired order before shoving them into an envelope. Even the most savvy publicist occasionally makes a drastic error, like leaving off the time of the event. If you discover a mistake of this nature, one that jeopardizes the success of your mailing, correct it! Fix your faux pas by issuing a follow-up release in an eye-catching color. Put corrections in writing. Do not make phone calls to add to or correct the information unless there is a time crunch. In the case of time considerations, either hand deliver a correction to the front desk or send a night letter. You might also phone the wire services to ask if they are running your event on their daybook. *Correct the error.*

With the media packet in the mail, it's time to celebrate. Congratulations! There is a joyous feeling of accomplishment and anticipation when you have plunked all those media packets into the mail and turn to face the exhilarating challenge that follows. Now relax. You have a few days to compile your list of telephone numbers and get ready for incoming calls that just might request you to give an interview or appear on radio or television.

8

Following Up
on Your Mailing

Unless you are promoting the hottest idea on the planet, you may wait for days without hearing one ring of the telephone. Don't be discouraged. Roll up your sleeves and get ready to let the world know you have arrived.

You are about to sell yourself to the media using your telephone marketing skills. Telemarketing—in this case thorough and consistent telephone follow-up—is an essential tool in any publicity campaign. During the five-day waiting period following your mailing you will have the time to begin preparations that will help you mount your telemarketing campaign with efficient ease.

Clients pay publicists big bucks for this essential talent: the ability to spend hours on the telephone repeating the same spiel with conviction and enraptured enthusiasm, as though it is the most wonderful idea on earth. It is this skill that enables you to convince media decision makers they need your story above all the others they are being offered.

The Elements of a Successful Media Telephone Pitch

Timing. Carefully choose the time for making your calls to media decision makers. If the show you are targeting is on the air at 2:00 p.m., it would be unwise to place your call at one o'clock or even noon. Immediately prior to airing any show or the printing of any periodical, the staff must focus on the deadlines they must meet. It is up to you to know when it is convenient for producers and editors to take your call. Your sensitivity to their time pressures will be appreciated.

The Telemarketing Setting. Choose a quiet place from which to make your calls. The professional tenor of your call contributes to your success. Noise, background music, or the presence of other chattering people will divide your attention. Chewing gum or eating food while speaking on the telephone is of course a no-no.

Being Prepared. You will need a list of the media outlets you intend to contact, along with the specific names and departments you are calling. It is a mistake to mix the call letters of one outlet with another or to confuse producers' names. Rattling sheets of paper while you stumble through mispronounced names does not endear you to the person you are trying to impress. Your notes should be arranged on a table or desk in front of you with the correct names and numbers immediately available.

One efficient method for charting telemarketing calls is to prepare a call sheet ahead of time. Your list should be categorized, noting media outlets on the left-hand side of the page and allowing plenty of space on the right for documenting your call results. Include such category headings as

RADIO: WEEKDAY MORNING, WEEKEND MORNING, DRIVE TIME, WEEK-DAY EVENING, WEEKEND EVENING, AFTERNOON

TELEVISION: TALK SHOWS, EVENING NEWS, PUBLIC SERVICE SHOWS

NEWSPAPERS: MORNING EDITIONS, AFTERNOON EDITIONS, WEEKLIES, SUNDAY MAGAZINES, MONTHLIES.

Within each of the above categories, rank your list of media outlets. The one with the highest audience rating (with the most listeners, viewers, and readers) becomes number one. Make your first calls to the periodicals and shows that are most appropriate for your particular story, and within that framework, those rated highest.

Keep consummate data on your conversations. Record even small details, such as producer/editor preferences, when it is best to call back, mutual acquaintances or interests, and any information that may facilitate establishing rapport with the decision maker.

Record each no, yes, and maybe. Make note of future opportunities for appearances. Try to get information about future trends in booking a show or periodical. When there is positive response to your pitch, note all relevant information, including the name of the person whom you will contact to coordinate your appearance or interview.

Have at your fingertips a call-back calendar for setting call-back dates and times, dates to mail additional information, and preinterview appointments.

Delivering Your Message with Pizzazz. The enthusiastic tone and rhythm of your voice is important to convincing the decision maker of your story's value. A jaded, half-hearted manner or a stilted delivery will defeat your purpose. Describing your subject matter with clarity and confidence is an essential part of the telemarketing process.

At least a day before making your calls and with your media release in

GOAL	CONVERSATION
MODE #1 GREET AND IDENTIFY THE DECISION MAKER Establish whom you are speaking with and whether the person has the authority to grant what you are asking.	TELEMARKETER "Hello, have I reached Sandra Cahn, the 'Noonday' producer?" DECISION MAKER "Yes, I'm Sandra. May I help you?" TELEMARKETER "I'm Lynn Edwards of Lifegrams. I'm interested in appearing on 'Noonday.' Do you book guests?" DECISION MAKER "Yes, what can I do for you?"
MODE #2 CLARIFY THE DECISION MAKER'S SITUATION Clarify! Does this decision maker have a moment to consider your request? How does he or she sound? If voice and manner are harried, establish a time when it would be more convenient. No one will respond favorably to your request if under pressure.	TELEMARKETER "Is this a good time for me to speak with you? I'd like to take about five minutes of your time to tell you about our event, which I feel is perfectly suited to your audience." DECISION MAKER "Uh, well, yes—I suppose so."
MODE #3 ESTABLISH YOUR PURPOSE Simply and briefly state your purpose. Inquire about whether she received your materials. She may elect to delay the discussion until she has them.	TELEMARKETER "As I mentioned, I'm certain our event is perfect for 'Noonday.' By the way, did you receive our media packet? It's a blue folder with Lifegram City Fair on the front." DECISION MAKER "Yes, I have it right here."

Continued

TELEMARKETING: STAGES OF THE CONVERSATION

GOAL	CONVERSATION
MODE #4 **TEST THE WATER—** **ESTABLISH RAPPORT** By eliciting the decision maker's opinion quickly, direct the conversation toward achieving your goal. Respond directly to her concerns.	TELEMARKETER "Oh, good. What did you think about our event? I hope you agree it will interest your audience."
	DECISION MAKER "Well, I don't feel it's right for the show. I do recall thumbing through your packet, but it didn't hit me as being really hot. However, I didn't spend a lot of time on it."
Briefly introduce relevant information. Make strong, succinct points.	TELEMARKETER "Our project is exciting and visual. Our May 18 visual fair for people who deliver Lifegrams is already attracting community support. The old-fashioned family circus will be the theme, with roving entertainers, colorful clowns, and incredible music from Firefly, the group on the cover of last week's Sunday magazine."
Call the question. You must determine whether you are on the right track.	TELEMARKETER "Does this sound as though it would interest your viewers?"
	DECISION MAKER "Well, it might be. Oh—but we had a similar segment a month ago. This might be too soon."
Diffuse the decision maker's doubt! As an aid to rapport, you might want to mention the segment of the show she refers to, if you have seen it. Indicate how what you are proposing is very different.	TELEMARKETER "Our event is unique in that city fathers will stage their favorite acts in costume. All of our performers will entertain in full costume."
MODE #5 **IMPART VALUE** Go for it! Whether your decision maker is totally negative, lukewarm, or mildly enthusiastic, now is the time to shoot for the moon.	TELEMARKETER "If you've never seen a grandmother on roller skates or human peanuts on stilts, this is the perfect story."

TELEMARKETER "We're presenting an exciting concept called Celebrating Life Events. We want to communicate the joy of progress within the family."	Of course you should now be using your rehearsed and timed spiel that runs no longer than two minutes.
TELEMARKETER "Birthdays, graduations, retirements are occasions for human telegrams."	Listen closely for reaction from the decision maker. Is she sputtering, breathing hard, trying to interrupt? Then let her. Allow her to question you. This indicates rising interest. Answer her questions without losing track of your goal.
TELEMARKETER "For an in-studio preview we would bring costumed performers and a sampling of the event."	
TELEMARKETER "Why, we might even convince one of the supervisors to do his juggling act."	
TELEMARKETER "The theme is especially fun because it gives adults an opportunity to reminisce about their childhood family celebrations."	Above all else, explain the project clearly, since people seldom select what they do not understand.
TELEMARKETER "Don't you agree that Life Events is a fascinating concept?" [Pause]	End with your question so that you elicit data about the direction of the decision maker's thoughts.
DECISION MAKER "Yes, but I'm not certain it's appropriate."	
TELEMARKETER "Just what are your concerns?"	Respond to the doubt; alleviate concerns.
DECISION MAKER "There are so many of these events, I'm not certain this is any different."	
TELEMARKETER "One very different aspect is the involvement of city officials. They are making a special effort because half the proceeds will be donated to help the handicapped."	

MODE #6
QUALIFY THE DECISION MAKER
Determine the conditions under which the decision maker would choose to cover the story.

TELEMARKETER "If we can show wide-based community support would you be interested in covering our story?"	
DECISION MAKER "Well, I'm just not sure."	

Continued

GOAL	CONVERSATION
MODE #7 IMPART SPECIFIC VALUE Emphasize the aspect of the story that intrigues the decision maker.	TELEMARKETER "Did I mention that Fred Winston, the National Father for last year, will be the master of ceremonies?"
End with a question. Remain keenly aware of the decision maker's feelings.	TELEMARKETER "Were you to cover the event, would you be arriving early morning or late afternoon?"
	DECISION MAKER "I'm not certain we would have the time. After all, you're located out near the park."
What are you hearing? Are you communicating the specific information that will move the decision maker toward saying yes? What unstated element is holding her back?	TELEMARKETER "Well, of course, one advantage is that our event will be in progress from 10 a.m. until 4 p.m. Spectacular sights will be available to tape at any time convenient for you."
MODE #8 DISCUSS SPECIFICS	DECISION MAKER "Looking at the datebook, I think we'd have to shoot early—well no—maybe 11 a.m. Would there be any audience at that time?"
	TELEMARKETER "Yes, we have a major performance with a city official at eleven."
Determine whether this is the time to pin down specifics or you should call later to settle the particulars.	TELEMARKETER "Shall we talk specifics or will I be contacted later?"
	DECISION MAKER "We'll need to be in touch with you a few days before the event for details."
Do not hang up without having a designated name and number for follow-up.	TELEMARKETER "Thanks so much for your time and consideration. I know you won't be disappointed. Is there a person I should contact to clarify details?"
	DECISION MAKER "Yes, Wanda Wash is the coordinator. Call her at 444-3333."

Determine whether the decision maker needs additional written material from you.

TELEMARKETER "Perhaps a program of events would be helpful."

DECISION MAKER "A letter confirming Winston's appearance would be helpful."

MODE #9
CLOSE

Arrest any remaining fears. Close with dispatch. Exhibit a professional manner that is warm and alluring and makes the decision maker feel comfortable with you and your story.

TELEMARKETER "If you have any questions, please call. And again, thanks so much for your time."

MODE #10
GENTLE PRESSURE:
TURNING NO INTO YES

Be willing to pursue success even into the jaws of defeat.

TELEMARKETER "I understand that you don't choose to cover my story (or have me as your guest), Ms. Cahn, but before I go, could I take one more minute of your time?"

DECISION MAKER "Well, all right."

Exert pressure without being obnoxious. Be careful to retain an open channel of communication.

TELEMARKETER "Whenever anyone of your respected professional status says a flat no to my request, I need to know the reason for the refusal so that I can correct any flaw in my own process. Can you be specific about why you refuse to cover my story?"

If the decision maker asks about an element of your event that you've overlooked, clarify.

TELEMARKETER "What can we do to meet your needs and be more appealing?"

If her refusal is a matter of timing or inappropriateness of subject matter, thank her and reserve the privilege of calling later.

TELEMARKETER "Thanks for your time. I'll be in touch when I have material that suits your needs better."

hand, devise a two-minute telephone marketing pitch that explains your product, service, or event. Keep in mind that words for a listener's ear must be provocative and descriptive. Rehearse your pitch until it becomes second nature to you. It is that kind of familiarity with the material that will allow you to execute a call and answer questions with assurance.

Assimilating the Telemarketing Process. Telemarketing is a process of selling: you are selling yourself. On page 69 is a format for successful telemarketing. Work with this process until you are able to glide easily from one mode to another. Knowing exactly where you are within this format and where you need to go to achieve your goal will help you master the art of telemarketing.

You will undoubtedly tailor this process to suit your own personality and the special needs of your promotional campaign. However, the structure outlined in the previous pages will serve as a guideline for developing your telemarketing skills.

This process is only a tool. What is most important is that you secure an interview or appearance. At any stage in the conversation that your decision maker indicates an acceptance of your pitch, halt! Stop! Close!

Check yourself during the course of the conversation. Are you explaining or saying much more than the decision maker wants to hear? Are you trampling on her "yes" to get your point across? Have you drowned her in words? When there is the slightest indication that she views your proposal with favor, abandon your sales pitch, go to Mode #8, and secure a commitment.

Your tasks are to determine her need, to match your product with her need, to arrest any fears, and to move into the close. All the elaborating in the world won't do any good if the decision maker doesn't need it. A green Rolls Royce isn't wonderful if you're shopping for a Mack truck.

The most valuable element for successful telemarketing is listening. At all times be aware of the decision maker's mood and direction of thought. You must analyze words, signs, and questions. Telemarketing requires you to be familiar enough with your material before you begin so that you can focus your total attention and energy on the pace and tone of your interaction.

Telemarketing Pitfalls

Telemarketers occasionally run into incredibly complex, puzzling, hilarious, and unsettling situations. One operating rule is to avoid disaster by preparing for it. To that end, pages 76 to 77 chart a few of the telemarketing pitfalls you might encounter and some solutions that can prevent trouble.

Under no circumstances should you argue with, insult, become hostile to, or threaten the decision maker. That kind of behavior can only work against your campaign. Media people are a tightly knit fraternity. If you develop a reputation for being difficult, it is you who will suffer.

By the same token, never confide information to the decision maker that you would not want to see printed on the front page of any newspaper. Once you have established rapport with the person you may be tempted to believe you have made a new friend who will empathize with your need and help you by covering your story. Wrong! Forget it!

However strange the situation, your aim is to move toward your goal in the most civil manner possible.

Media-Booking Etiquette

All the electronic and print media outlets within a defined area—a city such as your hometown—compose a "market." Within one market there may be two or even three competing early-morning or prime-time television or radio talk shows with similar formats. Do not attempt to book yourself on more than one of these shows within a six-week period without the express permission of the producers of each show. Cross-media fertilization can be a cardinal sin. Committing such a sin may block your access to the media for a long time.

Competition is fierce among media outlets within the same market. They do not like sharing topics or people. They thrive on exclusive stories to provide higher ratings. There are both spoken and unspoken rules of etiquette within the media: if you are to be successful at exercising your PR power, learn the rules of this game.

For example, the six-week exclusivity rule has many variations. Some shows in very small towns don't mind featuring the same guest on a competing station within the same week. Some shows in larger markets frown on booking guests who have appeared on competing shows within six weeks. National morning shows often prefer that you not double back to a competitor within six months of an appearance. Exceptions to this rule may be made for very famous stars, authors, and important politicians in such great demand that they can call their own shots.

The double-back considerations also apply when you seek interviews with competing newspapers or even different sections of the same newspaper. Editors tolerate the same story in two papers in one week or within the afternoon and morning editions on the same day only when there is a compelling justification and when they knowingly schedule them that way.

The lines of competition are not always visible or rational to the outsider, and the rules change. The best sources of information about the

WHAT IF:	IMMEDIATE SOLUTION	ALTERNATIVE ACTIONS
The decision maker is brusque, rude, and downright hostile.	Say "Thank you" and "Good-bye."	Look for someone else in the organization who might be interested in your story.
The decision maker did not receive your materials.	If the event date is imminent, ask whether she has a moment for you to explain your very special event or burning issue, which you feel is perfectly suited to her show or periodical. Attempt this only if the decision maker seems relaxed and receptive and assures you there is time to listen.	Offer to messenger or personally deliver the materials to her office. Time permitting, you can offer to remail the materials. Find out the best time to call back and discuss the event or issue after she has had a chance to look at the materials.
The decision maker says she absolutely hates your product or service. She has a friend who used it and was quite dissatisfied.	Tell her you are sorry. Offer to provide the product or service free of charge, or offer to send testimonials from ten people who have utilized what you offer and rave about it.	Later, do further follow-up calling. How did the decision maker like the sample product or service? Is she persuaded by the testimonials? Is she willing to reconsider? If not, so be it. Thank her for her consideration.
The decision maker has a negative view of your event based on past experience. "It stunk last year. Why should it be any different this year?" she growls.	Describe new aspects of the event. It is being organized by a different, more efficient group. The mayor endorses it. Ten celebrities are flying in for the event. Present written testimonials from notables who enjoyed it and community groups who desire coverage.	Persist, but do not get locked in a head-on struggle. In a subtle way, you may hint of the implied obligation to cover the event if the media outlet enjoys broad-based community support.

The decision maker requests unreasonable favors from you, such as ten tickets to your event for friends, or demands that you move your location or reschedule parts of the event.	Depending on the nature of the request, you might elect to acquiesce, if the request is not illegal, immoral, or fattening, and if you have no hopes for any other media coverage. One solution to the ticket request is to say "I didn't know that was a requirement. Shall I also send tickets to your news director and the general manager?"	Address the requested tickets to the news director or station with an enclosed letter addressed to a specific producer by name, noting that tickets are being sent at the request of the person who asked you for them. Of course, in response to irrational requests, you can write to the FCC and copy the letter to the station manager.
The decision maker launches into a tirade about your group and its philosophy, a "you people" type of dissertation that raises your blood pressure.	You are supportive of her individual right to a differing opinion. But isn't it station policy to include coverage for both sides of an issue?	Ask for the name of an executive producer or station manager to whom you can address an inquiry about policy. Do write the letter, or even better, send an overnight mailgram.
You can't get a word in edgewise. The decision maker is on a tangent, reminiscing about her youth, discussing her hobby, espousing her philosophy about your story.	Momentarily relinquish control. Go with the flow, but when you sense it won't be a harsh interruption, move back to your point before her time runs out and your opportunity to pitch your story is usurped by her obsession.	Since you share these interests in common, suggest getting together for lunch at a spot near the station. (This is hazardous, because if the person is of the opposite or even the same sex it can be misinterpreted. Never, never extend or accept invitations to meet in your apartment, the decision maker's apartment, or other private places.)

media booking etiquette are the producers and editors themselves. Be straightforward; simply ask what their policies are about guests.

Media Booking Strategy

When approaching shows within a media market, if there are two or more within the same time frame and with similar audiences and formats, make your first call to the one with the highest rating. If you are calling newspapers, make your first pitch to the one with the most readers. You can send your media packets to all outlets simultaneously, but you must follow media booking etiquette when making follow-up calls or when accepting bookings.

Information about ratings of media outlets will be available through your local community-access media organization or from the advertising department of each outlet. If you keep abreast of the news you no doubt already have some notion of who is top rated.

Let us suppose your first call is to "Good Morning, Pluto," a 10:00 a.m. local television talk show with the highest ratings in your area. The producer fancies both you and your topic but, refusing to commit, asks that you call back in three days.

Depending on your own time considerations, you elect either to wait three days or to call a competitor, the next most highly rated show on your list. If you are working against a deadline, obviously you can't afford to wait for undecided producers and editors to make up their minds.

One way of exerting pressure on decision makers is to imply that you are filling your schedule and want to give them an opportunity to be among those granted interviews. This tactic is sometimes used by savvy publicists to get initial commitments from the media. It is taking a risk, but when properly executed the ploy can result in a booking. When you can solidly point to one placement, other media outlets will likely follow suit.

Working your way down your calling list you will begin to discern a pattern. Scheduled appearances and rejections will form a road map to indicate those media outlets most—or least—likely to accept your bid. However, call each one. Set aside your hesitancy and call back the producers who have been "in conference" or "on another line" the first two or three times you tried to reach them. The PR game is full of surprises. Often it is the producer or editor you had entirely given up on who will be excited by your event and delighted to schedule an appearance.

If refused by number one, move on until you have secured interviews, even if they are with the throw-away shopper and the 4:00 a.m. community service show. One interview always leads to another. Media exposure resembles a pebble dropped into a pond: the waves begin in a tiny circle, then travel outward and get consistently bigger.

Avoiding Media Burnout

As you carry out your media telemarketing campaign, consider your long-range plan. Do not exert all your PR Power in one place at one time. Ask yourself what it is you hope to accomplish in one month, in three months, in six months. The novice may be subject to media burnout: blitz appearances on ten shows and periodicals in one two-week period followed by dead silence for life. These folks become has-beens even before they have had a decent start.

If you depend on people within a specific location to support your business, your goal is to build and sustain media momentum with periodic appearances and interviews. As you begin your campaign, keep in mind that a typical long-range plan might include four electronic media appearances and two newspaper interviews within a span of two or three months.

Realistically, producers and editors have the prerogative of scheduling you when they wish. You can, however, try to juggle dates and ask for bookings that suit your promotional campaign strategy. You can use one major event to generate media exposure over a three-month period. Talk shows will schedule your appearance to discuss plans for the event *before* it takes place. They might also consider having you on *after* the event, accompanied by taped coverage of its highlights from their own news departments.

As you schedule appearances, review your strategy: What is your goal? How does this specific appearance or interview fit into your plan? Be willing to adjust your campaign strategy to dovetail with reality.

Payola, Media Gifts, and Quashing Your PR Power

Often the question of whether to present media decision makers with gifts creates discomfort for publicity seekers and newly practicing publicists. It is indeed a delicate issue: witness the long-discussed "payola" scandal. Certainly, giving large gifts to sway a decision maker's opinion or to secure media exposure you wouldn't have received otherwise is to be avoided. On the other hand, to ignore the generosity of someone who goes out of his or her way to do you a favor is insensitive.

Perhaps you've heard of the now classic, outrageous media scandal that erupted when disk jockeys were found to be promoting records, songs, or performers for payola (the incident provoked the coining of the word). It rocked the media world and generated a wave of righteousness that still quells gift giving. Of course there is still graft, but in more subtle ways. As a novice in the business, you certainly don't want to create the slightest appearance of impropriety.

Somewhere between payola and rude behavior is the fine line of common courtesy. It is a code of behavior with which most publicists and decision makers find themselves quite comfortable. One benchmark for appropriate behavior is never to transact any kind of business or allow any words to come from your mouth that would make you uncomfortable if you saw them in print or heard them on the airwaves.

Many media outlets have a rule that anyone receiving a gift valued at more than twenty-five dollars must report it, though that rule is often overlooked. Those pedaling potential stories flood decision makers with theater tickets, free meals, clothing, jewelry, plane trips, pens, flowers, and all manner of bounty in the hope of persuading them to air or print a story.

Media professionals respond in various ways. Some will politely refuse even a stick of gum; others will grab without hesitation the key to your car, the shirt off your back, and your wallet.

The hubbub over payola has served to air the problem and to put it into perspective. Public access to the broadcast media is guaranteed by federal law, and nowhere does that law mention paying for the access. However, it is ultimately up to you to set parameters with which you feel comfortable. To reward someone who has granted you a favor, often an expensive favor, with a modest, impersonal, reasonably priced thank-you gift can be an appropriate gesture.

PART
THREE

Making It Big
on Your Own Stage

9

Preparing for Interviews and Appearances

Preparation is the key to achieving a successful media performance. Develop a written outline that covers the full range of material about which you may be questioned. List in order the points you wish to make during the time you will be on the air or in an interview. It is to your advantage to prepare yourself with a broad scope of information regarding your topic while keeping your priorities in mind. This dual anticipation is your insurance against failure.

Know all sides of your issue and be ready to discuss opposing points of view. You should be familiar with the topic you are presenting, especially negative points that might arise.

Research data reveal that audiences assimilate very little of what you say during an on-air appearance. There is evidence that people remember merely one specific bit of information conveyed during a forty-five-minute period. It is therefore essential that you be prepared to deliver your material in a way that emphasizes the most important aspect of your product or service.

Your goal is to deliver the kind of message that will leave audiences with a positive impression of you. They should conclude you are a sincere person whose product or service will provide them with value. Your demeanor and appearance should, above all else, leave the audience with a feeling that you are trustworthy.

Do not make the mistake of assuming that because you are a good speaker before your church membership or PTA you can ad lib or muddle through this presentation—you will find yourself being whisked off the stage without getting your message across. Time passes very quickly when you are on the hot seat. Having well-organized, cogent material at your fingertips will enable you to cope with any situation you might face.

It is your responsibility to research intriguing and news-related data pertaining to your topic. It is also up to you to provide photographs, video or audio tapes, maps, charts, or anything else that might enhance audience understanding and enjoyment.

When you have organized your material, rehearse it. It should be so indelibly etched on your mind that neither the accelerated pounding of your heart nor the nearby eruption of Mount Vesuvius will alter the flow of your performance. Give your outline to a friend and have her play the role of the host. Later, spend at least an hour visualizing the performance in great detail. Your play-acted and fantasy performances will give you a chance to practice thinking on your feet.

Adequate preparation provides you with the confidence to build a conversational bridge back to your main points. No matter how a host or fellow panelist chooses to discuss your topic you will be in command of the situation and able to diplomatically bridge your way to your specific area.

Hearing the answers roll off your tongue in a practice session will give you confidence on the air. If, however, you do make a mistake during an actual performance, proceed with dispatch. Keep rolling along, apologizing if appropriate, but staying focused on your goal. Even if it is a drastic error, apologize and forget it. Do not press the panic button. Do not let consternation about one mistake throw your entire performance off the track.

Be prepared for the interviewer to know nothing—or everything—about you, your product, or your book. Either being the case, you can then exhibit your best features. You'll be able to ask and answer your own questions. Do so without insulting the host or interviewer; maintain a kind and uncondescending manner.

Simply present your points. Use the phrase "People often ask me" or "Many people want to know" or "Often I am asked the question." In most cases the interviewer will pick up data as you reveal information and will sooner or later be able to ask questions of you.

Brief, punchy answers are the key to getting and keeping audience attention. Anecdotes get boring if they go on more than a minute. It takes a very skilled interviewee to unravel an anecdote in a way that is informative and entertaining. It is not a skill most people have. Therefore, avoid anecdotes during the first few interviews. As you become more adept at interview skills you will learn how to use anecdotes to punctuate your points.

Planning Your Periodical Interview

When you are scheduling an interview with a magazine or newspaper reporter, it's a good time to ask two questions that will help define the encounter: How long will the interview last? Is there anything I should bring? You may also have the opportunity to choose the interview site. If you choose your own home, be aware that the ambiance and decor may reveal information about you and your family that you do not want made public. Often a veteran reporter can pick up more information in a ten-minute tour of your home than you could write in a two-hundred-page book about yourself, your family, and your lifestyle.

If you decide to meet at your favorite restaurant, avoid ordering a large meal. Sloshing answers through strings of spaghetti or lettuce leaves does not portray the image you want to reflect. Energy needs to be focused on the brain rather than on the stomach.

Another option is to discuss the location with the interviewer and accept suggestions for a restaurant. However, choose a familiar place so you can be at ease. Whatever location is finally chosen, visit it prior to the interview day. Observe the premises with an eye toward its appropriateness for the occasion. How noisy is it? How comfortable will you be sitting and talking in a quiet and perhaps confidential manner?

Asking for a change of interview site is acceptable. In making such a request, however, be aware of your interviewer's time constraints. How close is his or her workplace to the alternate restaurant?

Preliminary scouting is time consuming but it can be very helpful in mastering the art of an effective interview. It is this kind of attention to detail that will ensure your success.

Preparing for a Periodical Interview

The major difference between a periodical interview and one for the airwaves is that you are likely to spend more time with the print interviewer. The reporter has an opportunity to probe issues in depth and to extract personal points of view that, again, you may not want made public.

Preparation for a periodical interview is virtually identical to that for an on-air appearance. You are being interviewed because you espouse a unique point of view or have information of interest to the audience. It is up to you to prepare yourself in a way that supports this contention. Have in mind an outline based on three main points of information you wish to discuss; this is an invaluable guide to conveying the right material to the interviewer.

With a casual setting and less pressure, you may be expected to elaborate on topics. The reporter with notebook in hand and more flexible time constraints can well afford to ask questions you don't want to answer and to do it several different ways. A print reporter is almost always very well versed in the topics you are being asked about. A well-seasoned print reporter will already know much about who you are, your points of view, and whether you have been written about before. He or she can press one computer button and get every article that has ever been written about you, your business, and your family history.

Being prepared will enable you to be relaxed and confident during this one-on-one session. Here, because you are person to person, it is especially beneficial to establish rapport. You cannot spend the hour thumbing through reams of paper or staring into a notebook. You may refer to, but not rely on, notes. Familiarity with your material will put you at ease and will allow you to speak freely.

Drawing parameters around the interview without erecting a line of confrontation is a skill you must learn if you are to be successful. For example, if you do not wish to give graphic details of your wife's political persuasions or your father-in-law's business dealings, you must respond to such questions without antagonizing the interviewer.

Patiently but firmly usher your interviewer away from the issue you find offensive. Hold the line with a gentle smile—and silence, if necessary. Nothing fuels a reporter's urge to dig into your background more than "No comment" or "I don't want to talk about that." It's like shooting off a gun and declaring the beginning of a war that you are not likely to win. If you remain calm you can arrest the reporter's urgent hunch that there is something to be uncovered by digging into your business. Behave as though you are undaunted, even when the question being asked scrapes your very soul.

Being interviewed by a professional who has all the time in the world requires real skill. You can learn it. Simply treat the reporter as the person he or she is: someone to whom you have recently been introduced. Don't for one moment believe that because this person is charming, wonderful, and delightful, he or she is your long-lost friend. Absolutely not. You know nothing about the reporter, but perhaps the reporter knows everything about you.

Keep all the goals and agendas in mind—both the reporter's and yours. The reporter has come to get a story, one that will sell newspapers. A boring story that does not have teeth will not please readers. So the reporter's goal is to glean enough of your inner tapestry to whet the reader's appetite.

Your goal is to reveal your inner passion, the adorable parts of yourself, your strength of character, and the wisdom that has brought you to where you are. This is not a time for talking about your frog qualities. It is prince and princess time. You are your own best publicist. No guilt-ridden confessions, please! Decide in advance just what parts of yourself you wish to reveal and avoid all last-minute decisions to go beyond that barrier.

Yes, reporters make wonderful friends because they are so interesting, so well read, so replete with life's tidbits. And yes, later you may become friends. But not now, not during these forty-five minutes that form the basis for a story the reporter will write for the world.

Please don't read this section and decide to adopt a false façade. The goal is to be the best of who you already are during these interviews. Be honest. Be careful. Don't worry. Most reporters are wonderful people; they are not out to trap you or to show you in a negative light. They are ordinary people doing a job. They are just like you. So don't plan to erect the kind of barrier that will prevent you from experiencing the presence of another human being.

Remember to wear clothing that makes you feel successful, well turned out, and comfortable. And, finally, relax. There is nothing more revealing about an interviewee than nervousness or tenseness. The question then becomes, why? Why are you behaving this way? The interviewer becomes uncomfortable and begins to look for the why of your behavior.

If it is your first time being interviewed, admit it. Simply say, "I'm rather nervous, this is my first interview. Please be gentle." Make a joke. Laughter is a universal tranquilizer. Your interview will be fun.

The best preparation of all is to be well rested, clear eyed, and energetic. Do not plan a marathon review period the night before; do not climb Mount Everest the day before; do not clean out your closets or reorganize your life just prior to your interview. Your personal well-being is reflected in your manner. If you are bleary eyed and hunched over with wrinkled brow and weary expression, your posture communicates more negative information than anything you could convey through conversation.

No matter what happens, no one interview can make or break your career. Cut the hysteria. You may have made an error. Yes, you might see it in print. No, perhaps the reporter didn't like you. No, maybe you didn't get your point across. But perhaps all those fears you have are needless. Maybe, just maybe, you did everything right. At least you took a giant step by getting under your belt the lessons you'll need to be victorious when bigger and better interview opportunities come along.

Planning Your Television or Radio Appearance

If you are scheduled to appear on radio or television you will be assigned a contact person. This person is your link to the talk-show host or hosts, the producer, the director, and the technicians—the entire production team that makes the show come together. The contact person's task is to facilitate your comfort with your physical surroundings and to assist you in being a success on the air.

Establish rapport with this person and plan, if possible, to meet in advance. It is essential that you understand and trust each other if the details surrounding your guest shot are to flow smoothly. Compile a list of questions pertaining to your appearance and thoroughly discuss your concerns.

Sample Questions for Your Contact Person

- How long will I be on the air?
- Will my appearance be taped or live? (Taped indicates you can "stop tape," should there be a mistake, and redo it. Live means you are on the air from the moment of your appearance.) Will there be an audience?
- Will I be alone or a member of a panel or a participant in a debate? If a member of a panel, who are the other guests? If a debate, will my point of view respond to or be countered by someone else? If so, who? (Have the contact person provide you with a biography of that person and a position paper.)
- What time am I expected to be at the studio?
- How long should I allow for the entire process?
- Does the studio provide a makeup person?
- Will the regular host be present that day?
- Am I expected to provide props, charts, photographs, and additional film or tape?
- May I visit in advance the specific set on which I will be appearing? May I be a member of the audience during the week prior to my appearance?
- Is special attire suggested? In view of your equipment, do you have suggestions about color selections to be avoided?
- Do you have special instructions not touched on in these questions?
- Do you need additional packets of material for the host?
- Will the station provide transportation to and from the show? (Unless you are booked on a major show, it is unlikely. However, some stations provide limousine service to and from the studio especially for early morning and late night shows. Do not push for a limo if it is not a customary practice.) If I am to drive, is there a provision for parking?
- How often may I refer to my product or service? (For example, will they be electronically printing your name and title or position across your chest as you speak? How would you like that designation to read?)

Take notes so you can avoid unnecessary harassment of your contact person. Get your questions answered all at once. But if there is the slightest doubt in your mind about what is expected of you, don't hesitate to telephone again. Be cordial, be brief, but be persistent in getting the information you need to perform at your peak.

Clarifying Your Role as a Guest

One major problem that often arises is a misunderstanding of the role of an on-air guest. Ask your media contact how the show is billing you. Who do they say you are? Are you the resident expert on a certain topic? Are you a member of a group espousing a radical point of view? Are you presenting one side of an issue in opposition to your own minister, priest, or rabbi?

In the course of your conversation with the contact person inquire about the kinds of questions you will be expected to answer. Although it is inappropriate to request a specific list of questions, in some instances they may be offered to you. Your inquiry should be only about the direction and the tone of the discussion.

If at any time you are vague about the station's arrangements, it is up to you to clarify them. Not to do so is to sabotage your appearance. An interview in which the host or hostess has different expectations from the guest can be unpleasant, if not devastating.

Previewing Your Surroundings

When making a media appearance on radio or television you may be distracted by the unfamiliar surroundings. Lights, cameras, gadgets, people in motion, and odd trappings, along with the faces of strangers in an audience, can be nerve-racking. Acknowledging the likelihood of last-minute panic and dealing with it beforehand is a giant step toward perfecting your performance.

Ask your contact person for a tour of the studio. An ideal arrangement is to observe the show from the studio audience prior to your appearance. Avoid, if possible, the suggestion that you arrive early and preview the space on the day of your guest appearance. That is inconvenient and impractical. The preview tour should be carried out well in advance of your big day.

If it is not possible to visit prior to your guest shot, arrive a half hour earlier than scheduled on the day of your interview. Your goal will be to observe and become comfortable with your surroundings. Be honest with your contact. Explain what you would like to do and ask for help. Wandering about a studio unescorted probably won't be tolerated, and besides, it can be an unpleasant experience.

Dressing for Media Success

The clothing you wear on television should be chosen to enhance your desired image. If you are a fashion designer, now is the time to show your skill. If you are a businessperson, the picture should be appropriately professional and tailored. If you are a dancer or entertainer, creative flair counts.

There are, however, base guidelines for all appearances. The eye of the television camera somehow magnifies tenfold what it records, so whatever you choose will present an exaggerated picture of yourself. This is not the time for outrageous dress but rather a time to be subtle, understated, and above all else, appropriate. Unless you want your image portrayed as the best hooker, criminal, clown, or character in town, follow these rules and dress conservatively. The executive, dress-for-success style is appropriate for most of your television appearances.

The image you present will be judged by hundreds, if not thousands, of people. During the first moment they see you their mental cameras will snap a picture; based on that picture, each will make a decision whether to trust and believe you, to laugh aloud, or to disregard you. If you are uncertain about how you should dress, seek help from a fashion consultant. However, a media appearance is not the occasion for purchasing new and daring clothing. Wear what is familiar and comfortable. While on the air you will be seated beneath hot lights. Choose clothing that will be comfortable in a room that is at least seventy degrees. Check to see whether the studio is air-conditioned. If it is, then you have the option of wearing heavier-weight clothing.

Both white and black clothing should be avoided. Never choose oddball prints, large polka dots, bold stripes, or harsh colors. Avoid clashing and clanging jewelry. The audience should be able to focus attention on you—not your clothing and accessories.

As a rule of thumb, choose primary colors or rich burgundies, navies, and earth tones. Monochromatic color schemes are desirable. A brief review of any of the dress-for-success books will provide ample ideas of appropriate dress for both men and women.

This clothing advice applies to radio as well as to television, and also to interviews with periodical reporters. Treat each occasion as though you were going for a job interview. You are conveying a message about who you are and the integrity of your product or service. How do you wish to be remembered when you call back for a second request to appear?

Media Preparation Overkill

Don't be the victim of media preparation overkill. MPO is a disease that sneaks up on frightened guests and sabotages those with the best intentions. Those who labor long hours through the night before an appearance are courting disaster. A prescription for success is to *be yourself. Relax!*

During the days prior to your media appearance or periodical interview, *pamper* yourself. A sauna, hot tub, massage, and even a few days away at the beach can add to your personal charisma. After all, you are a star! Stars look wonderful. Bulging red-streaked eyes and sagging round shoulders won't do much for your image. Your goal is to energize yourself so that you can inspire and delight the audience. Keep in mind how those television cameras pick up and exaggerate every bit of visual data you transmit.

Although it may be true, as experts say, that audiences don't remember most of the information you present, the overall impression you make will probably stick with them. If you are dragging and listless it will be reflected in your media performance. You cannot attract clients on three hours of sleep. They will be repulsed by the possibility that if they buy your product or use your service they may end up looking as listless as you do.

As many disasters result from preparation overkill as from lack of preparation. You don't have to become a talking encyclopedia. A know-it-all guest who sounds like a doctoral candidate but who looks like dirty laundry and won't let anyone else get a word in edgewise is a real turn-off.

An interview, whether with a periodical reporter or talk-show host, is, after all, an exchange. All your answers should be brief and to the point. The flow of conversation runs rather like a verbal sharing with a friend.

Do your personal best to prepare yourself and your material, then relax. No one ever expired from an in-person or on-the-air interview. The ultimate preparation is to be comfortable with yourself. Approach your new adventure with a professional posture, a sense of humor, and a willingness to learn from whatever mistakes you make.

10

On the Hot Seat–
You're a Star

No matter what the media opportunity—radio, television, or periodical interview—you are expected to show up on time. There is no excuse for late arrivals, especially when you are a guest on the airwaves. If there is an unavoidable accident or family crisis, telephone as soon as possible. Even in the wake of a catastrophe, missed appointments for interviews and appearances without notice are unforgivable. If you are ill twenty-four hours before a talk show, cancel. Do not wait until the day of your scheduled appearance to decide you can't make it.

An effective media guest is alert and confident. Lucidity is mandatory. Don't even think of having a drink or altering your consciousness with any sort of drug before you appear. In all cases, you are also expected to tell the truth. To be wonderful, alluring, or theatrical is desirable, but to lie in order to achieve that effect is unforgivable. Media representatives may exaggerate to achieve the kind of drama needed to sustain audience interest, but you don't have that right: you are an invited guest.

You are expected to charm, delight, inform, and excite an audience. All this personality must come through as you deal with the fact that thousands of people will be analyzing, discussing, and refuting your opinions. Throughout the process, keep in mind that being an effective media guest is hard work. It is work that requires preparation and practice if you are to attain the perfection you seek.

Whenever you speak to a reporter or a talk-show host, be aware that the interviewer believes what you are saying is for public dissemination. When you are interviewed by a media representative on tape, you have the choice of giving information that spans from A to Z. If you give that full range of information, you give the interviewer the power to decide to use information from C through H. Ask yourself whether the information revealed along that spectrum is what you want the world to know. If not, why did you say it? Control what is written or said about you by controlling your tongue. Reveal only the information you wish to see in print or hear on the airwaves.

Double-check to be certain any allegations you make are accurate. Credit your sources when making controversial statements. Be well versed in the opposing points of view. Do not give specific psychological, medical, or legal advice without qualifying it, or you may be held legally responsible for that advice.

No matter what the nature of your media opportunity, you are expected to be cordial to your fellow guests, to the producers, and to the host. After all, you are a guest.

Always send thank-you notes to those involved in making your venture a success. A small but thoughtful gift is also appropriate. Going to great lengths to discover that the producer of a certain talk show collects baseball cards or that your favorite columnist likes pictures of old movie stars is time consuming but it may be rewarding.

The media individuals to whom you show consideration will greet your next request for an interview with that same consideration.

Delivering an Effective Media Performance

It's the morning of your electronic media performance. With a final glance in the mirror, you exit the front door and head for the studio. Of course you are a bit frightened. Take heart! The only way to allay your fears and become media-savvy is to take your place on the hot seat.

The following checklist will help you deal with the little details that might cause last-minute panic:

- Leave early. Allow plenty of time to get to the station. Plan to arrive earlier than scheduled.
- Consider taking someone supportive with you—an assistant, secretary, or mate. This person should be a confident, relaxed individual who makes you feel good about yourself.
- Do not drive. Jangled nerves caused by heavy traffic and the hassle of parking are not a prelude to your best performance. If the studio doesn't provide transportation, have a friend drive. Or take a taxi.
- Take along extra materials, such as media packets and brochures.
- Take your checklist of points to get across to the audience.
- Check the kind of jewelry you are wearing. Will it clank and jingle against the microphone?
- Remember to bring any necessary props, photos, film, tape, or documents.
- Provide for taping your appearance. It is unlikely that the television or radio station will provide you with tapes.

The Rules of Etiquette for TV

When you arrive at the television station you will be greeted by your contact person, who will take you immediately to the green room. This room derives its name from the holding room in a theater. It is simply a comfortable area in close proximity to the set where you will appear. Rest rooms and the makeup area are usually nearby. During your time here you will have an opportunity to relax, to meet other participants on the show, and to discuss any last-minute details regarding your appearance.

- Do not make panicked revisions in your game plan.
- Do not glue yourself to your notes.
- Do not alter the three major points you have outlined.
- Socialize! Relax! Enjoy being a star!

If the station provides a makeup artist you will be escorted to a room to receive the full treatment. You too, fellows! If you think the makeup artist is painting you up to resemble Godzilla or the neighborhood hooker, say so. You can object; it's your face. The makeup is, of course, heavier than that to which you are accustomed. However, it shouldn't be objectionable to you.

After being made up you will return to the green room, where often three or four other guests are waiting. If you are to appear as part of a panel you will be introduced to the others and encouraged to socialize with them. Your aim is to get a clear understanding of how your major points relate to the main course of the conversation. Assimilate tips about what will be expected from you during the on-camera discussion. Above all else, concentrate on retaining peak energy and relaxed confidence.

As you wait, a contact person may offer a variety of foods. This is not the time to clog your throat or soil your clothing. Sugar and caffeine can alter your mood and bring on a case of the jangles. Hot lemon water, herbal tea, or room-temperature water are preferable refreshments at this time. Don't consider alcohol. You may think a couple of drinks would be relaxing, but alcohol can have disastrous effects under the hot lights. Do not drink alcohol of any kind within four hours before your performance.

At no time during the green-room stay should you indulge in unguarded chatter. Any inclination to confide your innermost longings to your contact person or host should be squelched. These people are professional friendlies but they're not your friends.

The host may meet briefly with guests just prior to the show. This meeting often takes place in the green room. It will provide you with an opportunity to become acquainted with your interviewer. Your first goal is to convey the proper pronunciation of your name. Then, briefly explain the nature of your product or service. At this time you may be given more instructions about the nature of the on-stage discussion.

It may happen that you do not meet the interviewer or host until he or she comes to get you during a commercial break. In this case you have only a brief moment to get onto the set and into place. As you hurry to your seat, make your name and purpose understood in three sentences or less. Extend a hand and establish eye contact. Inquire whether your media packet is needed. If the interviewer already has your materials, ask whether there are any questions.

As you take your place on the set and prepare to go live, you may be frightened. Move ahead. A slight bit of stark fear in the pit of the stomach provides the impetus for a good performance. Fear will help you focus, if you harness it properly.

Live and In Person in the TV Studio

At the same time you are making your acquaintance with the host, settle yourself into your seat. Take nothing for granted. Make inquiries. Are you seated in the designated spot? Is your microphone properly attached? A producer or technician should attach your mike and check it for sound.

Be careful what you say and how you move from this point on. Avoid unguarded chatter. The possibility always exists that there are hot mikes transmitting signals over the airwaves.

Ladies, make sure that your knees are covered. Gentlemen, drop your trouser legs over your socks. Make yourself comfortable. Look around. Take note of people and things. Notice which of the technicians appear to be significant in assisting you with your task. Be aware of people affiliated with the show's production. Cast a surveying glance at the audience. Acknowledge your supporters—aunts, uncles, friends, and significant others—with a smile and a nod. To safeguard your concentration, however, from this point on avoid establishing eye contact with anyone in the audience, especially people you know.

Note cameras with red lights flickering on and off (tally lights signaling hot, or live, cameras). Throughout the performance, you will focus your attention on the host. Once on the air do not attempt to follow the red light or look into the camera. Be aware that the cameras will dolly (move) around you. Do not let this motion distract your attention.

Notice the monitors. Your image will be reflected on those screens. Indulge yourself. Look all you want before you go on the air. Once you've begun your performance, ignore them. To peer constantly at yourself distracts your attention and distorts your facial expression as you react to what you see.

Notice the person called the floor director. He or she wears a set of headphones linked to the camera and communicates with the show's director. The director, who observes what's going on from the control room, dictates the ebb and flow of the show's activity and conversation. He is in charge of movement and conversation on the set. The floor director is your link to that director. The floor director will sometimes signal you to end your comments, as the segment comes to a close, by twisting a fist left to right in swift motion (indicating fifteen seconds left), then by extending all ten fingers, withdrawing one with the passing of each second.

Do not ignore the floor director's signals. The cardinal sin in television is to violate time constraints. Each second means big bucks to someone, either the station owner or the advertiser. You will not be looked upon kindly if you rattle on past either the host's or the floor director's efforts to stop you.

Once you've been introduced, look alive. What makes conversation interesting is its pace and rhythm. No magic bunny is going to tap you on the shoulder to tell you it's your turn to talk. Be alert! Although you do not want to rudely interrupt your host or step on anyone's lines, you do want to get your word in. You do want to look enthusiastic and energetic. If your topic is an especially sad or sobering one, tone it down a bit; basically, all talk shows present an upbeat, fast-moving conversation.

Concentration is the key to a successful performance. Listen closely to the questions and answer in a way that allows you to put across your major points. Do not relinquish total power to the host. Your answers can sway the direction of the conversation. Seize opportunities to guide the conversation into channels that lead back to your points. (Remember your preparations in the previous chapter.)

At the same time, avoid usurping the conversation. Long-winded descriptions and dissertations are forbidden. Complex stories and anecdotes that are the least bit off-color are out. One rule for the novice TV guest is to avoid using anecdotes or jokes. Concise answers are the key to success.

If the host veers too far off your topic, you should be quick to provide a bridge back to the area of your expertise. Some talk-show guests believe they must always answer a question if it is asked. Not so. If the host asks a probing question that you feel treads on your privacy, you can politely direct the conversation elsewhere.

For example:

HOST: So, Mr. Jackson, I see here in your book on divorce you are suggesting equal custody. Tell me, how many times have you been divorced?

GUEST: You know, multiple divorce is a particularly interesting issue where children are involved. It means, of course, they must cope with many sets of parents with differing viewpoints.

HOST: But I asked how many times you've been divorced.

GUEST: Well, I wouldn't want all my former mates to converge on me here. I do know that there are now mediating services that facilitate the divorce process.

You don't want to be accused of being evasive. However, only as a last resort would you look the host in the eye as you say, "I prefer not to go into my personal life." Try to keep the conversation flowing while circumventing the probing question.

Do Not Overhype Your Product or Service

Your repeated references to your product or service can be obnoxious and may result in your being exiled from the media world. Occasionally during the conversation you might refer to your book, your salad dressing, your videotape rental shop, your massage parlor, your relationship seminar, your legal or medical practice. But the references must be subtle and general in nature:

"We at Fluffstead Associates like to believe that our promotional services differ in that..."

"Our massage at Heaven House is therapeutic because..."

"Oh, yes, I talk about wife-beating in my book, *Open Marriages, Closed Doors.*"

Waving signs giving the date of your seminar, clutching at your book, or perching your videotapes on the arm of your chair as you repeat clearly and slowly their brand names is a no-no. Heavy-handed hyping will get you ousted.

Allow the host to take the lead in these matters. Your contact person may have approved superimposing letters on the screen for the name of your book, location of your seminar, address of your store, or a telephone number where you may be reached. That issue having been explored, it should now be clear to you just how far you can go at hyping yourself and still be considered an appropriate guest for this particular show.

There may be occasions when the host allows an open, full-tilt discussion about your product or service. Go for it. In this instance you are allowed to promote at your best, but don't overdo.

As your appearance winds to a close, a graceful exit can ensure a return invitation. Wrapping up the segment with upbeat advice leaves the viewer satiated. As you exit, whether at a commercial break or at the end of the show, do not linger. Take your cue from the host. Don't chitchat. A simple compliment and thank you is appropriate. "I've enjoyed this experience. You made it really easy for me," or "You were as delightful in person as you are on the air. Thank you."

If the show is taped, get information about when the show will air. Ask how you can retrieve props or other materials from your contact person. Leave your telephone number in case there are further inquiries. Send thank-you notes to the contact person, producer, and talk-show host.

Radio Interviews

As you enter the studio, do not make assumptions. Often there are several microphones at the desk. Ask where you are to sit. Locate your "cough button" (the button you press to cut off the mike if you feel an overwhelming urge to cough or to clear your throat). Double-check for jangling jewelry, loose papers, clanking buttons, or anything that might rattle against the microphone. In anticipation of call-ins, you may need a headphone set. Since you may be on the air for long periods of time, you will want a glass of room-temperature water. Because of fear of accidents, studios often do not permit coffee, tea, or food near the equipment.

The profile of a desirable radio guest is much the same as for television. But radio requires much more of your energy. It requires you to titillate the imagination of the listeners; they have no pictures on which to rely. You provide those pictures with your words. As you prepare your notes for a radio appearance, consider speaking with a bit more punch than you would for television. Make your descriptions more vivid.

The same rules apply for a successful interview on radio as on television. Your presentation must be focused, stimulating, and informative. Of course, conditions may thwart your best efforts; see pages 100 to 101 for a table of worst-case scenarios and options for regaining momentum.

Radio guests are often expected to interact with listeners who call in, so prepare yourself for a range of logical, strange, and irrational questions. Call-ins can hamper your effort to get your main points across if you have not outlined your points in advance. A long-winded caller who is prepared to debate the hour away can be a menace to your game plan. If the host is a professional, he or she will not allow this to happen. If the host does not intercede, firmly but politely turn the caller into a fan by answering the questions directly and briefly.

On radio, anecdotes are more appropriate. Still, they must be kept clean and short. The tone of your voice and cadence of your speech should convey an upbeat mood, unless of course you are doing a session on grief; even then, remember that you can approach any subject from a positive perspective.

Keep a note pad at your side to jot down points to which you must respond. Write down key words that form bridges to the points you have come to present.

Although newcomers tend to be more at ease on radio because they are heard but not seen, do not underestimate the skill it takes to maintain an informative, upbeat, and energetic dialogue. In a way, you have to give more of yourself on radio. You must convince an audience of your value and integrity with your words and the sound of your voice.

Above all else, you have a right to preserve your dignity, to be treated fairly and with respect. Never sit still for a situation that violates your self-esteem. Remember, you are valuable. No promotional opportunity is worth letting someone insult or mistreat you. The fact is, you have a unique gift that you are sharing. If your gifts are not welcomed and honored, they should be withdrawn.

If you ever face one of those rare but extremely unpleasant situations in which you are being taken advantage of or mistreated, walk away. There is always life beyond the hot seat.

Almost always, however, you will find that being on the hot seat is stimulating and fun. Once you've had the experience, you'll want many, many more.

Periodical Interviews

In most cases the reporter is not coming to do a hard-hitting investigative story or even a review; the piece—if the paper decides to run it—will be a feature story, emphasizing the human interest angle. Of course, something you say or do may change the focus—don't reveal graft or corruption—but there is no need to be afraid of the print reporter.

The reporter may bring a tape recorder as a backup for note-taking. This is standard procedure. If the reporter asks whether it is all right to tape the interview, of course you should say yes. Realize, though, that the interview begins when you meet the reporter, not when the tape recorder is turned on or the notebook is at the ready.

You should also be clear in advance whether a photographer is coming or whether the reporter plans to take pictures. If a photographer arrives with the reporter the picture taking will most likely occur first, so the photographer can go on to another assignment. If the reporter carries a camera, the photo schedule may be more flexible.

A reporter is a professional, trained to elicit and analyze information. This person will most likely form an opinion and write a story colored by

WHAT IF:	OPTION #1	OPTION #2
You get a miserable cold that hits moments before you are due at the station. Gagging and coughing, you can hardly speak.	Call the host and decline to appear. Offer a substitute who is prepared to speak on the same topic, someone who can do a good job. Offer to reschedule at their convenience.	Call the host. Explain your problem. Let the host handle getting a new person.
The talk-show host alters the topic at the last moment.	Convince the host to reverse the decision, or if you are prepared to discuss it, forge ahead. Use specific points to tunnel your way back to your own topic whenever appropriate.	If the suggested topic is ludicrous and you will feel like an idiot discussing it, leave! Say you are not prepared for the change. While you would love to participate, you don't want to embarrass anyone. You wish to reschedule.
The host mispronounces your name badly as you are introduced.	Correct the person immediately. Be polite. Perhaps you can find a way to use it to make a point.	Wait until the commercial break and tell the host how to pronounce it.
The host talks too much. You can't get a word in edgewise.	Politely but firmly step on his or her lines. Unless it will result in the eruption of World War III, break into the conversation.	Wait until the commercial break. Remind the person that you have a few points you need to get across.
You are on the air with a panel. You cannot get a word in.	Go for it. Seize your time. Do it with dignity, but do it!	At the break, ask the moderator to clarify ground rules. Explain that not much is being accomplished with the free-for-all.
Your time is running out and you have not yet said what you came to say because the moderator hasn't asked the right question.	Ask and answer your own question. "People most often want to know" or "I am so often asked" or "You haven't asked the most-often-asked question yet."	Interject, "One fact the audience might find interesting is . . ."

Situation	Response	Alternative
You are on, but your time is reduced by the talkativeness of a flamboyant guest on the air before you.	Get to the heart of your material. Pick the most important point and stick to it.	After the show, ask to be rescheduled.
You have uncontrollable sneezing on the air.	Take your leave. Apologize and return later, if possible. The host will cover for you.	
The host alters the topic midway through an on-the-air interview.	Tread water. Gently turn the conversation back to your topic.	Be direct. Say "You've changed the topic and I am unprepared. I don't want to give misinformation."
You have a hostile call-in while on the radio.	Try to reason with the person, but only for an instant. "I don't think this discussion is going to resolve anything" is a good exit line. Do not offer your services or try to heal this person of anger or dementia on the air.	Let the host handle it.
You are asked a question you are unable to answer.	Say "I don't know the answer to that one."	Say "That's a good question and I'll have to look up the latest information. A related question that I've just researched is..."
The moderator suddenly runs out of time. You are not going to be on the show after all. You have waited in the green room. Friends and family are viewing and listening.	Show disappointment, but turn major effort toward rescheduling. Be polite!	

the resulting point of view. Do not have unguarded chats with the reporter. Any temptation to begin a sentence with "Off the record" should be resisted. Maintain a distance and do not cross the invisible shield that must remain between you and the reporter.

Stick to the point. Keep in mind why the interview was arranged. Stick to your outline. The reporter's questions set a tone for this interview. If you are uncomfortable with the reporter's viewpoint, advise him or her that you are prepared to discuss the topic from a specific perspective.

Look the reporter in the eye. Establish rapport. Be aware of what messages you are conveying with your body language. If you are meeting your reporter in a restaurant, remember that satiating your appetites for food and publicity at the same time will not work. Voracious eating will distract you from your goals. Espousing your point of view through mounds of pasta can be hazardous to your image. Order sparsely and push the fork around your plate as you focus on your task.

If the interview is in your home, do not bombard the reporter with cats, kids, spouse, relatives, and neighbors. Designate a quiet space and quiet time for the interview. Do not give a heart-rending tour of the house, explaining family heirlooms and artifacts collected on trips abroad, unless the reporter specifically requests it. And even then, be certain it is relevant to your story.

The interview should last no more than an hour. If you take up time with useless dialogue and tours, the point of the interview may be missed. Avoid lingering, intimate, friendly chats.

Toward the end, mentally review the points you have made. Have you said what you wanted to tell the reporter? If you see your story in print, will you be pleased? If not, you may speak up and tell your interviewer your concern that important points have been left out and that you wish to be certain he or she has a clear view of where you stand.

11

When and How to Call
a Media Conference

The scheduled occasion to which reporters and cameras are invited to witness and report a story is called a media conference. It may also be referred to as either a news conference or a press conference. Inviting the media implies that the action or announcement is of great import. Announcing a media conference is seen as a request to inform as many people as possible as quickly as possible about your news story.

Media assignment editors assume conferences are to be reserved for earthshaking announcements. Examples of appropriate occasions for calling a media conference are an elected politician making a long-awaited decision that affects his or her constituency, a movie star arriving in town to reopen a local theater, a group of citizens banding together to demand a stoplight at a dangerous intersection, or people staving off the eviction of the elderly from a particular building.

The subject of a media conference must be of significant interest to large numbers of people, although the interest can be commercial. Major manufacturers frequently call such conferences to announce a new product or service. But it is unwise to assume a small-business owner can utilize this same vehicle to promote products or services.

An exception may arise if you can form a link between your subject and broad-based community interests. An example would be a bicycle shop providing newly developed cycles for youths on a peace mission through Iron Curtain countries. But even with such an intriguing news hook, this kind of promotional gimmick could be seen as suspect and may be bypassed by media decision makers.

Avoid needless or frivolous media conferences. Be clear about the ramifications of holding such a conference when your topic does not have proper news value. If you summon the media without justification, you risk having them totally ignore future occasions when legitimate coverage of your story is warranted.

If you conclude that your topic rates a media conference, the occasion can result in an abundance of radio, television, and newspaper coverage for the twenty-four-hour period following the conference. You can also expect follow-up appearances on talk shows. When handled properly, a media conference can be a very useful springboard for the dissemination of your views.

Presenting an Effective Media Conference

Because television news is visually oriented, pictures must tell the story. In your media conference plan include provisions for visuals and on-location demonstrations. Consider how you will demonstrate the urgency of your plight or the excitement of your triumph.

Consider holding the conference at the scene of the injustice, giving the photographers an opportunity for dramatic visuals. If elderly people are being put upon, where are they? Provide a picture of their dilemma and emotional pain. If consumers are being ripped off, show us the shoddy quality of goods for which they are being overcharged. If the citizens in your block want a stoplight to prevent traffic accidents, let's see a victim of the latest accident (on crutches and in a cast, please) standing at the dangerous intersection for the media to tape and photograph.

The dread of every TV journalist is a media conference full of "talking heads." Because such conferences are considered boring and unappealing to viewers, they are treated with little regard. Often television stations send "camera-only" (without a reporter) to a series of these media conferences to "shoot thirty seconds and pick up written information." This means the broadcast will include a polite blurb read during the news show by a disinterested anchor as pictures on tape run by faster than a speeding bullet. Blink and you miss the story. To avoid being relegated to the talking-heads heap, plan a visual presentation of your media conference and announce your plans to assignment editors.

If you're too outrageous with your visuals, you may be precluding coverage except for a few sleazy outlets. Your goal is not only to attract attention but also to garner public support.

If you can't find a reasonable method for visually dramatizing at least some aspect of your presentation, reevaluate. Would you be better off pursuing a wave of appearances on local talk shows than being relegated to the thirty-second treatment?

Perhaps the most important factor in ensuring the success of your media conference is preventing negative publicity. If there was ever an occasion that could work to your detriment, this is it. It is the journalist's task to explore and perhaps exploit some aspect of your topic that will interest an audience. It is the provocative, the scandalous, and the intriguing that attracts and holds public attention. If you have the slightest notion that your media conference harbors elements that can provide material for daytime soaps, don't do it!

Ask yourself whether you can maintain complete control over the information disseminated during your media conference. Are you certain that other participants in the event will stick to the agreed-upon game plan? If not, devise a different vehicle for getting your message across.

If properly planned and executed, conducting a media conference can be a stimulating and exciting venture. It is, however, not something you want to relegate to your spare time or leave for a last-minute task. It requires a written plan of action and your undivided attention to details.

Preparing for a Media Conference

Refine your presentation both verbally and visually to highlight one major point. Assume that the actual time you will have on the air, whether on radio or television news, is approximately ninety seconds. Focus on the essential message you want to get across to the audience in that time.

You will be able to convey a very small amount of information during the course of your conference. Within the scope of time allotted for it—no more than thirty minutes—you cannot successfully present a massive body of ideas. If you try to get too many points across you will only confuse the reporters, and they will fail to get across to the audience the message you desire.

In addition, if you present myriad ideas during your media conference you give the reporters present the latitude to choose what they feel is most important. To ensure they convey an accurate message that reflects your viewpoint, stick to your theme. Impart only information that explains, supports, and elaborates your message.

Plan to introduce your materials with your opening statement, which is a brief, two-to-three-minute presentation explaining your view of the issues. List three specific points that elaborate your main theme. These will provide a framework for the discussion to follow. Have in mind questions that you may be asked by the media. Outline your answers and have those notes at your side.

Reporters' questions may steer you off the track. Be prepared to answer in an informative manner that reveals still more facts in support of your viewpoint. No matter what the momentary distraction, always use as few words as possible to bridge your way back to your main point. Outline and rehearse the answers to questions you anticipate, so that you can keep your responses brief and cogent.

Selecting a Spokesperson

A key element in an effective media conference is the spokesperson. If you elect not to fulfill this role yourself, choose someone who is articulate, personable, well informed, attractive, and appealing. Keep in mind that this person will represent the image, and hence the message, you wish to convey to the public. Choose a person with polished speaking skills who, ideally, has prior experience of media conferences.

Do not make the drastic mistake of choosing several spokespersons to officiate during your media conference. Multiple speakers can deliver a message that confuses both the reporters and the audience. The most effective method for delivering your message is with one strong speaker.

If you must choose two speakers, delineate their roles long before the actual conference begins. Be certain they know which portion of the issue each is to discuss. Have the representatives rehearse so that their statements coordinate and they do not step on each other's lines or appear to be in conflict.

Another consideration when choosing a speaker is the person's reputation. Ask yourself whether this individual, by virtue of prior actions, has a reputation with the media. Will reporters be able to draw any negative conclusions from the mere fact that you have chosen this person to represent your cause? Will reporters become so fascinated with the speaker as an individual celebrity that they ignore altogether the theme of the conference?

The spokesperson you choose must be skilled at answering reporters' questions. Savvy reporters will have done their homework. With the advantage of research assistants and high-speed information systems, they have an abundance of data at their fingertips. This means your spokesperson must be fast at thinking on his or her feet.

Choosing the Appropriate Time and Place

The time you choose for your media conference can affect the probability of its success. Review the calendars maintained by your city government, chamber of commerce, newspapers, and community groups to determine whether any events are planned on the date you anticipate conducting your media conference. Avoid heavily scheduled dates on which competing events are likely to lure the media away from your story.

Note the time schedules of local news shows. Knowing the precise time of the newscasts will enable you to schedule your media conference at a time convenient to the reporters. Do not schedule a media conference within two hours before a newscast you target.

Also be aware of deadlines for local newspapers. If you are trying to place your story in a specific edition, be considerate of its time requirements. If you are hoping for coverage by a weekly or monthly periodical, investigate the lead time required for including your story.

Do not plan your conference at a time that is routinely chosen by city officials to hold their media conferences. In many cities, Monday morning at nine is the time for official media conferences. Choose instead a mid-week morning or early afternoon when nothing else of great importance is taking place. Tuesday and Thursday mornings are usually good times to hold a media conference. Do not choose Friday morning unless it is your only option. Friday is often reserved by news types for closing out the week, using stories done earlier, and for airing happy magazine-format stories.

Although you may have done a thorough job of investigating possible time conflicts, you always risk competition from breaking news stories or natural disasters. A breaking news story always takes precedence over whatever else is going on. Once one occurs, there is very little you can do to compete. However, advance telephone calls to your local fire and police departments can reveal information about days and times they are most busy. You can avoid those times as you make your plans.

The time it takes to cover a story is always a consideration for any assignment editor, so the location of your media conference can determine whether you receive adequate coverage. If your conference is miles away from the studio and you plan a 4:00 p.m. time slot, it is unlikely reporters will jeopardize the quality of their 5:00 newscast to cover your event. Locating your conference so that it is convenient to the media makes the commute easier and adds incentive for reporters to attend.

Do not be locked into the notion that a media conference need be held in a dreary room with people seated behind a long desk giving speeches. To the contrary: if you have a choice, always lean toward a more flamboyant and dramatic setting. Choose a spot that will enhance your presentation and aid in visualizing your point.

Choose a location that provides the proper ambience for a professional media conference. A tiny, musty space next door to a rehearsing rock band will not be appreciated. Be certain you consider such elements as available light, adequate electrical outlets, rest rooms, and parking facilities. If a crew has the choice of where they will go (and many times they do), they are more likely to choose the story located in the most pleasant environment.

Select a media conference room that provides an enclosed space protected from intrusion by passersby. There should be enough space to accommodate everyone who participates—on both sides of the podium. Electronic media crews often have three people: reporter, camera person, and sound technician. Allow ample space for them and all their equipment.

An ideal room is one that can be reduced or expanded with portable dividers. It is unwise to stage your media conference in a large, drafty hall when only three participants and two media crews may show up. This space would emphasize the lack of attendance.

A hotel conference room is usually a workable space. Often it can be quickly reduced or expanded with movable room dividers. These facilities also boast adequate parking and telephones, as well as nearby rest rooms and refreshments.

Avoiding Crowds

Do not freely distribute invitations to your media conference. Crowd scenes are unnecessarily noisy and distract from what otherwise might be a smoothly functioning event. Invite people critically necessary to staging your media conference. The presence of relatives, dogs, kids, neighbors, and "old Phil who hopes to get a glimpse of his favorite newscaster" can interfere with your doing a professional job.

If the media conference is being sponsored by a large group, avoid having all board members and, once again, multiple spokespersons present. Instead, have the group vote for two people who will represent them. Other board members or associates should be forbidden to communicate with the media. Unless the presence of a large number of people demonstrates support for an issue or individual, avoid crowds.

Your Media Conference Release

Your release for the media conference should follow the same format as the basic media release (see Chapter Five). One major difference, however, is that it will contain fewer facts about the issue being addressed. A release announcing a media conference is somewhat like an invitation to a birthday party. Tell guests that a wonderful event is taking place, but don't spoil the surprise by describing it in great detail.

List the occasion for the invitation, its time, and its location. Give a provocative hint about the issue in question and only sparse but alluring details about your reason for inviting the press. Give enough of your story to entice but not so much that reporters will be able to write a story without attending your conference.

There is one school of thought that advises requesting RSVPs. Seldom do members of the working press know precisely which assignments they will cover until the day before the event, however, so an advance reservation list is hard to maintain.

Don't Give Away Your Story

Many novices make the mistake of discussing their stories prior to the event. As they deliver their releases or call to inquire whether the material has been received they enthusiastically unlatch the floodgates of description, and details pour out. Then they are surprised when no one shows up. Of course no one will come. Why should anyone? News is just what the word implies—something new. Leaking parts of your story will doom your media conference. Nobody wants old news.

Your Media Conference Mailing

Mailing your materials at least fifteen days but not more than twenty-one days prior to the conference is preferable. The requirements for a successful mailing under these circumstances are the same as those spelled out in Chapter Seven. The clarity and brevity of your materials, along with their visual appeal, dictate how seriously decision makers will consider covering your story.

Follow up the mailing with a preliminary call in which you simply inquire whether the packets were received. This call is brief. Give a name and number for media representatives to call should they have any questions. At this time you are not soliciting their interest or trying to get a definite answer about whether they will attend. However, during these conversations you may glean some indication about assignment editors' attitudes toward your conference.

Three days before the press conference make follow-up calls to elicit information about the media's attitudes toward covering the conference. Identify the proper decision makers—usually the assignment editor or show producer. Find out whether they have your materials. After answering any questions they may have, ask if they are planning to cover your conference.

Do not be discouraged if decision makers refuse to commit to a positive answer. It is unlikely they will know for certain whether they will cover your conference until the last moment. A major storm, breaking news, or other unforeseen events can affect their decision. Consequently, a yes even hours before your media conference can turn into a no. A commitment to cover is not what you are trying for at this point. What you want instead is an indication of their *willingness* to cover. If the indications are negative, use persuasive arguments to change their attitudes (see Chapter Eight).

On the day before your media conference telephone the wire services in your area. See that they have included the announcement of your media conference in the schedule of events for that day.

On the morning of your media conference telephone all outlets in your area. Begin as early as 6:00 a.m. During a brief conversation, remind the assignment editor that your media conference is taking place. At this time it is inappropriate for you to get into a long and involved conversation.

However, do keep in mind that it is your last opportunity to get their attention and perhaps their coverage.

Some organizations and individuals emphasize the importance of their conferences and remind the assignment people of their occurrence by sending telegrams on the morning of the event. This is a clever action but there are risks involved. Be careful not to antagonize the decision makers with overkill.

Some publicists advocate calling assignment editors an hour prior to the media conference to remind them again of the importance of covering the story. But this kind of action in some cases persuades media representatives to avoid your story at all costs. It's up to you to be sensitive to the mood and attitude of the people with whom you are dealing.

Briefing Sheets and Updated Media Releases

Within twenty-four hours before your conference create briefing sheets and updated media releases. The briefing sheet is a one-sheet document, sometimes called a media brief or backgrounder, that states concisely the facts relating to issues being presented at your media conference. You may include a position statement, which gives your point of view on the issues. Briefing sheets should be distributed the day of the event.

Briefing sheets are prepared to give reporters a quick overview of the issues and to provide relevant background or other information that may not be covered in the media conference. Include particularly difficult spellings and pronunciations of the names of people, places, and things.

Updated media releases are reserved for those occasions when there have been significant changes in events or actions just prior to the media conference. The new information is placed in the first sentence. It is virtually a rewrite of your original release with a bit of spice added. If properly written, this updated release can also generate renewed interest in your topic. These releases can be handed out as reporters arrive or, if the event's timing allows, mailed three days prior to the conference.

Instant Media Conferences

Should the occasion arise for you to call a media conference on very short notice, first consider these three questions: Does your topic warrant the media changing their already tight schedules to add your last-minute event? Will the information you hope to disseminate be outdated three weeks hence? Are you prepared to execute all the details necessary to bring about a successful event?

If the answer to all three questions is yes, go for it! Deliver your media release, either in person or by messenger, to local assignment editors. You may want to send mailgrams or telegrams. Sending your media release by wire accentuates the urgency of your media conference.

Within two hours of distributing your release telephone all media outlets including wire services to find out whether your material has reached the right decision makers. If your conference is the next day, make certain wire services are carrying it on their daily calendars. Of course, you are wise to do early morning follow-up calling on the day of your conference to sample media attitudes about coverage.

When reporters receive notification of a media conference they will often try to wrangle a preinterview with the subject. They will promise you everything, including the moon, for the privilege of an exclusive (being the first one to break your news story). Granting such exclusives can work to your detriment. It can be a real turn-off to the other reporters you hope will attend your conference. Every reporter is looking for a fresh story or a fresh angle on an old story. From the reporter's perspective it is somewhat demeaning to be part of the masses covering a conference, particularly after another reporter has scooped the exclusive. Seldom will you serve your interests if you acquiesce to granting preinterviews.

If someone affiliated with your project should leak aspects of your story prior to the conference, it is in your best interest to respond to calls from reporters. Explain that the information leaked was only a small aspect of what is a grand story that they can ill afford to miss.

Often journalists try to get an edge on the story by calling to ask that you confirm or deny a controversial accusation relating to the issue you plan to discuss at your conference. Be coy! Be persistent in your refusal to answer their questions, but do so in a polite way. Point to the media conference as a time when you will reveal scintillating details of the story.

Occasionally a publicist can use a news leak as an inducement to the media for wider coverage. But successfully utilizing that kind of ploy takes someone with experience and solid media contacts. You are better off not talking to reporters about your media-conference issues until after the event takes place.

Setting Up Space for Your Media Conference

If at all possible, have access to the space for your media conference at least twenty-four hours ahead of the event to allow time for proper setup. For the cameras, the speaker's table should have a backdrop that is uncluttered and will not distract the eye. Highly reflective surfaces, such as mirrors, windows, and marble walls, should be eliminated.

If natural light is available, it should be directed in a way that compliments the spokesperson. Speakers should not sit with their backs toward a window, because photographers will have difficulty getting the proper exposure. Preferably, speakers should be seated so they can be lighted from the side and front. If natural lighting is not possible, an arrangement of strategically placed lamps may be substituted. Overhead light should never be harsh or glaring. There must be sufficient light so it is easy to discern your speaker's facial features from virtually any spot in the room.

Reserve enough seating for at least two thirds of the media invited. Also take into account space needed for any other people who will be present for the occasion.

Check the room for "booby traps," such as ringing telephones, squeaky chairs, collapsing tables, music on house speakers, proximity to police and fire stations, and neighboring conventions. Identify any inconvenience that might interfere with your conference or else it may later embarrass you.

Make one final check of the little details that, if left to fate, could cause you to tear your hair out at the last minute. Find out if there will be a jazz band playing next door or street repair with a jackhammer. These events could put a real damper on your proceedings.

Pay close attention to the general cleanliness of the area. Cobwebs hanging from the ceiling say something about how much you value your efforts. If you plan to have refreshments, make certain there is adequate counter space to hold them. Also, do not overload space allotted for displaying additional media material.

Gather all maps, charts, and other visual displays you will use during your conference and place them exactly where you will need them. If pictures are to be mounted on the wall, double check to make certain there are provisions for hanging them. If you want your corporate seal, organizational insignia, or company logo on the front of the podium, cover the hotel's seal with your own.

Any organizational tasks that can be performed ahead of time should be done as far in advance as possible. Then you can be relaxed and deliver your message at peak performance.

Coffee, Tea, or Milk?

Whether to serve refreshments at your media conference depends on the nature of your topic and the appropriateness of the facility you are using. If a particular food relates to the issue you are discussing, then having reporters sample it is in order. If you are conducting your media conference to mark the opening of a new restaurant, serving refreshments that reflect your menu is expected.

Ask yourself how food service would enhance your efforts at achieving your conference goal. Consider the extra burden such provisions could place on you. Would food preparation and service compromise the success of your conference by distracting your attention from other important details?

Coffee, tea, croissants, and fruit can be appealing to the media during early morning hours, when they may have missed breakfast. But a major consideration must be whether you have space that allows you to separate the food service from the room where the conference is taking place. Clanging spoons in coffee cups do not make an appropriate context for attracting and holding the attention of the media.

Sometimes the food service itself adds provocative tidbits to an otherwise boring news story. Both the abundance offered by the community group pleading poverty and the sumptuous spread served by the slick politician preaching belt tightening can make great—and unwanted—news copy.

Unless you are totally convinced food service will enhance your event, forgo it. When in doubt, do without!

Conducting Your Media Conference

Designate one of your people to act as host, greeting reporters and camera operators as they arrive. This person's sole responsibility is to interact with media representatives, make them comfortable, and provide answers to their questions. He or she should be sophisticated, should present a professional image, and should have a working knowledge of the media and an ability to identify reporters and their affiliations. (This person usually carries a clipboard with pen and pad for taking media representatives' names and affiliations.) If you are having refreshments prior to the official presentation, this person is responsible for directing the media to the service.

The host must, above all else, be charming. There is something to be said for charm in any situation but especially in this one, where reporters can, with the stroke of a pen, rain torrents on your parade.

A moderator should conduct your media conference. This person's job will be to guide the flow of the conversation and act as intermediary between the spokesperson and the reporters. The choice of moderator should be guided by the impression you hope to make on media representatives. The moderator and the host may be the same person.

Here is a standard opening statement used by moderators:

Good morning, I'm Gloria Lightner, the public information officer for the Pluto State Fair. Welcome, ladies and gentlemen. I'd like to thank you for coming out today, especially considering the rain. Our topic this afternoon is the format and plan of this summer's Pluto State Fair. Speaking with you this afternoon and answering any questions you may have are the State Fair Association president, Mr. Fred Azxariro; that's spelled A-Z-X-A-R-I-R-O, listed on your briefing sheet; and Ms. Nancy Wykman, who is the citizens' chairperson of fair activities. Your briefing update also includes a copy of the opening statement by Mr. Azxariro.

At this point, the spokesperson delivers the opening statement. Following that, the moderator opens the floor to questions from reporters. If any question in any way becomes difficult for the spokesperson, the moderator steps in to field it. He or she may do so in a diplomatic way, but the end result is to prevent any reporter from confronting or antagonizing the spokesperson.

When thirty minutes have elapsed or when the pace of questions slows to a halt, whichever comes first, the moderator calls for the final question. Following that question, the structured part of the media conference is ended with "Thank you, ladies and gentlemen. If you have further questions, Mr. Azxariro will be available following this session."

There will be instances in which a reporter stands and belligerently protests that he or she didn't get a question in. The moderator can placate the reporter by repeating the announcement—that the spokesperson will be available afterward to answer questions.

Whether the spokesperson moderates or has someone else do it, there are bound to be negative questions. The strategy in response is to avoid antagonizing the perpetrator. Rather, answer the question as succinctly and politely as possible. If that does not ease the situation, perhaps promise to speak with the questioner later. As diplomatically as possible, quickly direct attention to the next important words or action.

Avoiding Post-Conference Carelessness

Immediately following the media conference reporters often swarm like locusts, looking for that one provocative tidbit that will make their ordinary story a scandalous scoop. It is during this rather chaotic time that inappropriate and even negative information may be revealed.

Sometimes it is that offhand information rather than your intended focus that is seized upon. Well-meaning but unknowing associates or a cousin from West Virginia may inadvertently say something that should not be divulged. It is too late to stop such revelations after they hit the press. The time to do it is beforehand. Advise everyone involved with your group to be polite but closemouthed and to direct all inquiries to the designated speakers.

What to Do If the Reporters Don't Show

So you've given a party and nobody came. Take heart! It happens to the best of us. Even professional publicists have had to face an absence of media. If absolutely no one shows up, issue a brief media release including the statement made by the speaker.

Telephone the local media and wire services and offer to fax them a brief statement about the event. Deliver, by messenger, updated media releases along with appropriate photographs. These efforts very often result in your acquiring at least some coverage.

For your own education, ask at least three of those media representatives the reason they chose not to attend your conference. This kind of feedback can provide information that will help your next media conference.

What to Do If Only One or Two Media People Attend

When only one reporter attends your media conference, carry on as though all is well. You may elect to present your material in a less formal manner by forgoing the opening statement and allowing the reporter to begin by asking questions.

Deliver your message to the best of your ability. Follow-up calling, along with delivery of media releases and statements immediately afterward, can sometimes generate limited coverage.

Follow-up Pays Handsome Dividends

Someone representing you or the organization can do follow-up checking to see which electronic or print media failed to attend the conference. One approach to soliciting more coverage is to bombard these people with a media release updated from your original one that details the major focus of your conference. Also include copies of statements made and responses to significant questions.

During follow-up calls to media outlets, repeat a brief update with a polite reference to the fact that you are providing this service because they were unable to attend your conference. Offer to fax a statement and to put them in touch with the spokesperson for a phone interview, should they desire one.

The caller's attitude during this follow-up campaign is one of a helpful informer rather than of a pushy and demanding adversary. It will not serve you in the long run to intimidate, insult, or pressure any of the people with whom you speak.

Depending on the nature of your media-conference issues, you may be able to garner additional exposure by calling local talk shows and pitching the producers. Refer to the splendid coverage during the past few days on what is demonstrably a topic of interest to audiences.

If you learn nothing else from this chapter, you need to understand that a media conference can be a lethal weapon when used against you by a reporter out for a provocative story. When a media conference is good, it's really good. But when it is bad, it's oh so awful. Executing a successful event requires immense energy and effort. When you can make it work, it can pay off in enormous promotional dividends.

12

Freebies:
Creating Promotional Opportunities

Promotional events attract media coverage and familiarize the public with your product, service, and location. No matter what the nature of your business, you can create a media event that will bring you free publicity on the airwaves and in print. To get the publicity you desire, you may have to generate a reason for media coverage: that reason is called a news peg.

News pegs are made—not born. A successful promotional event requires that you be willing to devise a detailed plan and to assume some risk.

The event should relate to your business in a way that enhances people's understanding of the service or product you offer. The first step is to consider your options. Is your business more suited to a grand opening, anniversary celebration, community-involvement project, or political clambake? Pick a reason: any reason will do as long as it has potential for luring people, reporters, cameras, and more sales.

Creating Events that Make News

Successful promotional events can range from outstanding to outrageous. You may have to reach far afield to find just the right one for your purposes. Let's say, for example, that you are a realtor with a prime property to sell. Consider sponsoring a play-a-thon to benefit your favorite charity. Erect a playground complete with swings and miniature golf course on the property. Commandeer a local celebrity to host. Invite movers and shakers to pay admission to cavort in front of the cameras. Call the event the night of "Adult Games." The best player at children's games wins $100 for a favorite charity and a 10 percent discount on the property, should the winner desire to purchase it.

This doozy can attract the rich and famous to your site, giving you an opportunity to rub elbows with folks who can readily afford your prices. Do a super job of promoting this folderol. The media will turn out in droves to photograph and write about the antics of local celebrities. At the same time, they will also be showing pictures of your property and talking about the location, the view, and other attributes.

As an added attraction, you might even decide to auction off your property during the event. Not only might you earn commission dollars, but in the crowd of people you've gathered you will no doubt discover several other potential clients.

It's an outrageous idea! But it's often the outrageous idea that works. Here are a few other events that have been successful promotional vehicles. (Chapter Eighteen lists 100 inspirations for all kinds of businesses.)

A cookie store located in a prime area for foot traffic but also amid stiff competition needed to rev up business. The owner decided to give each customer the chance to guess how many chocolate chips were in a huge jar placed on the counter. The person giving the closest estimate would win a $1,000 donation for a favorite charity. Reporters filmed and reported the noon crowds shouting their best estimates.

To encourage the media to return to witness the check-giving ceremony, the store hired a chorus dressed in turn-of-the-century costumes; as the chorus sang Christmas carols, the media filmed the event and told audiences about the wonderful cookie lady whose generous donations were helping others.

Another promotional scheme that worked very well for a newly opened restaurant was a benefit using city officials and local celebrities as waiters. These hotshots served meals during the lunch hour of opening day. Guests on that day paid triple the regular lunch prices, with the proceeds going to a city-sponsored summer jobs program. Of course, having been showered with media releases that dropped the names of participants, the media flocked to see the bigwigs in service.

If you are promoting your video rental shop, why not sponsor a biannual classical movie evening? Give a major prize, perhaps a VCR and a membership in the rental club, to the person who comes dressed in the best period or character-lookalike costume.

Piggybacking onto Events that Promote Your Cause

Piggybacking is a convenient way to stage a promotional event. Find a great event already in progress, preferably one that boasts a history of success, and tie into it. You will become part of an ongoing success, thereby ensuring your own triumph.

Examples of such events or actions might be involvement with a United Way project, a Red Cross drive, your local Girl Scouts, the Kiwanis, or any group that has achieved momentum and public recognition. Investigate what is going on with your children's school PTA. Look about for some great annual festival already in progress. If you are a member of any of these groups, consider events you may be spearheading as a prime source for your own promotional vehicle.

Offer to provide the uniforms for a Little League team; donate food for the retarded adults marathon; provide a booth in your local fair; sponsor the premier party for a theater opening; create a float for the annual St. Patrick's Day parade. These kinds of endeavors provide access to new groups who are potential customers.

Search for a community group that needs a location for its event. If it is in concert with your goals, offer your business space. Your generosity will create publicity for your business as new people come to your place. After they become comfortable with you and the setting, they will return when they need what you are selling. When the media show up to cover the event, make sure your company logo and product identification are prominently displayed.

To get a look at the piggybacking technique at its peak, observe politicians during campaigns. They show up uninvited at church bingo parties, bar mitzvahs, and numerous other functions. They then take over and make the event their own, as few of the attendees realize exactly what's going on. You can't be quite that bold and have the same positive effect, but opportunities will fall your way, and you can be ready to make the best of them.

Avoiding the Pitfalls in Planning Promotional Events

The biggest mistake that can occur in planning a promotional event is to underestimate the cost of staging it while overestimating the returns. The key to avoiding such trauma is to devise a line-item budget, anticipating every imaginable cost. Then estimate the greatest possible amount you can receive from direct sales to a large crowd. Also estimate the amount you will earn if you draw only a very small crowd. Work within a realistic budget and make realistic projections. Don't gamble with money that you can't afford to lose.

Careful planning and attention to detail are essential. First, make a preliminary budget. It will act as a guide to the event's expenses. Start by choosing the optimum circumstances in which you would like to stage your event. Telephone each of the facilities or retailers you want to use and get precise prices for their goods and services. Build in a miscellaneous fund for the last-minute items that inevitably crop up.

If your first choice for optimum staging is too expensive, do an analysis of your second choice. Have a third alternative if need be.

Your budget will become the pivotal core of a working and expanding plan for your event. As you clarify details, it will change to reflect the ongoing status of your expenditures. Having this budget tool will enable you to keep a close check on how you are spending your money.

Next, evaluate your purpose for sponsoring the event. What are your realistic expectations: New, long-term customers? An immediate hike in income from sales? An increase in goodwill? All three? The event you choose to create should be in concert with your expected return and your budget.

The novice's next big mistake is to underestimate the time it takes to handle all the details that underlie a successful event. Compile a task chart. This is a document that lists, step-by-step, all the functions needed to execute an event right down to the most minute detail.

Begin by listing every task associated with the function you plan. Pencil in an estimate of the time required to complete each one. As you add the total hours, days, and even weeks, ask yourself whether you can expend this much time and energy without jeopardizing the structure of your business.

How many friends can you count on to take over nitty-gritty tasks? And even if they help, can you afford to expend the time to manage such a project?

One pitfall that plagues novices and veterans alike is the tendency to see these promotional events as occasions to socialize with old friends. No! This is business. Determine exactly how you will attract new people who are potential customers. If, indeed, old friends are invited, the price of their admission should be to bring a guest who is a prospective buyer for your goods or services.

Bigger Is Not Better

Do not deceive yourself into thinking that the biggest and most flamboyant event will garner the most media attention or the most customer interest. To the contrary, sometimes it's the very small but well thought out event that yields the greatest return.

For example, in the promotion of ceramic picture plates, the simple idea of forming exchange clubs has helped to skyrocket what was only a hobby into a multi-million-dollar business. Now folks meet at yearly conventions to exchange, barter, and promote the plates grandma used to hang on her dining-room wall. One woman, who started collecting plates in her kitchen three years ago, earned three hundred thousand dollars last year through such promotions.

Usually it is the idea that is easiest for you to execute that will be most effective in accomplishing your goals.

If you are not having the event on your own premises, visit each of the locations you are considering. If you are renting equipment or furniture, preview the specific items you will use to check their condition. Do not make major decisions during telephone calls.

Whether you are contracting for a rock band or for equipment or location rental, put all agreements in writing. Make sure to cover such important specifics as the time and place of delivery, setup and knock-down times, and liability insurance.

If you are offering food, pay close attention to preparation and quality, and be aware of the health department regulations. When hiring a caterer, make a specific menu and then get three bids. Compose a written agreement outlining the caterer's responsibility to provide utensils, setup, and cleanup. Be certain your contractual agreement includes the number of people to be served and the estimated portions the caterer will be providing.

Whether you hire assistants or use volunteers, draw up a task sheet of assignments with specific completion dates for each task. Periodically check on progress so you can avoid last-minute surprises.

Leave nothing to chance. Discipline and attention to detail are your safety nets for a smoothly operating event—the kind that will win friends and influence potential customers.

The Who, What, When, and Where of Your Event

It is impossible to have a promotional event without a featured attraction: a star. That star may be a person, place, or thing. You take a great risk when you stage an event without some special attraction and assume people will show up. Even in a small town, there are so many events these days that folks can afford to be choosy about how they will spend their time and money.

Consider whether your star attraction will draw the media to your event. Will the place or thing you are featuring have universal appeal to a wide variety of people?

The stars that draw crowds range from local celebrities to merry-go-rounds to fancy gadgets that do fancy things. No matter what the occasion, analyze your star attraction. Will it compel people to choose your event over others? Will it make them feel as though they have gotten full value for the time, energy, and perhaps dollars they invested in attending your event?

It is wise to consider featuring someone or something that comes accompanied by a built-in audience. By designating a star with a loyal following you automatically have a core group upon which to build large attendance.

For example, if you have an event theme focused on fashion, invite members of a local sorority, a teacher's association, or the Junior League to model. By doing so you create a ready-made audience of their husbands, sons, mothers, and friends who will show up out of loyalty.

When considering a star for your event, do not make the assumption that your choice must always be the most expensive, most important, or most sought after. You can do something simple but creative, such as celebrating Christmas in July.

Location is an equally crucial factor in attracting an audience. If you have a wonderfully magical event but you are located on the far side of town or in an unsafe neighborhood, your expected attendance can dwindle to a loyal few. Why should folks travel a long distance or risk life and limb to experience your wiggling, walking widget when there are so many other attractions down the block? You will want to stage your event in a convenient location that offers ample parking.

Have your promotional event on the premises where you sell your product or service, if there is adequate space and an appealing ambience. People who attend the event are more likely to return to purchase because they have become familiar with the setting. When your place of business is featured on television or in newspapers, people will gravitate to it rather than to an unfamiliar setting.

As you build your experience with promotional events, you will become confident enough to alter your approach by planning events that target different audiences. You will also be able to tailor an event to a larger audience, one that might not fit comfortably on your premises. Off-premises events can also serve to enhance your public image and attract new customers.

In some instances, a location can be the star attraction: a bingo festival at the Space Needle, a hike near a waterfall, a tea dance at the town's most chic hotel, or a tour of a socialite's home. In each of these cases you attract an audience because of the location of your event. Is your location appealing? Is it a place you would choose to go?

Another ploy that works well is to choose a location that comes with a ready-made audience. Try having an event in a financial-district park on a sunny day, a square where business people congregate, a popular watering hole for young professionals, or any other location that attracts people who might be interested in what you're offering.

The time of day that you stage the event is a key factor in determining whether it will be successful. Are your prospective patrons swinging singles, family folks, or working people? Is it likely they might need time after work to freshen up before attending? Might a weekend event be more convenient than a week night? When is it most convenient for them to attend?

One event involved the most elegant Los Angeles theater opening of the year. Stars had vowed to be present; everything seemed to be in place. But one week before the event the sponsor realized it was scheduled on Rosh Hashanah, one of the two holiest days of the year for Jewish people. There would be lots of empty seats. The planners had erred by not being sensitive to the needs of their patrons. Don't you be caught in the same bind. Know your audience!

Promoting Your Promotional Event

When inviting the media to cover your promotional event, follow the same procedure described in previous chapters. In particular, draw from the information in Chapter Eleven on media conferences. The media release for your event should be light, upbeat, and cheery.

Your invitation to the media should give a few enticing details but not so much information that reporters can phone in their stories without attending. Mentioning the names of famous people who will be attending may attract reporters who might otherwise not attend.

Although in most cases a promotional event will be a feature story, point out the news value of your story. Emphasize the appeal of the star attraction, the location, the particular actions or activities that will make for appealing pictures. Whether you focus on value to humanity, an occasion for family togetherness, or an opportunity for community involvement, the way you package your story is important. You must view it from the perspective of the media decision maker. How is it going to look or sound on the air? What will it be like in print? Will it attract an audience?

Avoid creating the impression that you are holding your event solely to promote your product or service.

Taking Out Insurance against Disaster

Whenever possible, determine beforehand how well attended your event will be. Make follow-up calls to get responses to your invitations and estimate the size of the crowd. When in doubt—"paper the house." Call up all the people you know and invite them! For an event, unlike a media conference, it's better to have too many people than not enough.

Every experienced event-giver knows the feeling of having to paper the house. They've had to fill a room or event with people who weren't necessarily invited, don't want to be there, and won't serve the purpose for which the event is given. Yet it's better than explaining to reporters why nobody bothered to show up at your grand ball. Papering can be a necessary tactic to protect your reputation. Don't be upset if you catch yourself having to do it—once. You can always find a group of scout mothers or church or club members and give them special invitations.

To paper a house or event effectively, you need to know at least forty-eight hours in advance that your potential audience is a bust. At that point, reduce the price of tickets for the elderly, the handicapped, teenagers, mothers accompanied by children, children accompanied by pets....
If you can afford to do so, hire a crew to distribute last-minute fliers announcing the coming attraction. If these measures don't create positive results, it's time to employ even more drastic methods. Set up a telephone tree. Call everyone you know. Have them call everyone they know. Do whatever it takes to display warm bodies enjoying your event.

While papering the house can avoid a disaster in the eyes of the press, you should realize that for future events something needs to be done differently. Evaluate carefully whether and how you want to handle your next promotion.

Little Extras that Make Success

As your big day draws near, assign someone to manage the details of the actual event. If you are the host or hostess, you must be free to pay attention to the media. Novices sometimes make the error of trying to officiate over their events and attend to details at the same time. It's a mistake.

When greeting the media, follow the procedures described in Chapter Eleven for media conferences. If your event is spread over a large area, such as a fair, you will need several people to conduct media guests around it and to point out the important activities. If your event runs over a period of hours, reporters and cameras will arrive at varying times; keep in mind that you must approach the reporter who arrives five minutes before the end of the event with the same enthusiasm that you displayed to those who arrived early.

No matter what the nature of the event, always remember the aspects that you feel are most important to promote. Direct the media and your guests to the ones especially planned to intrigue them.

Think of the people who attend as your personal guests. This attitude will assist you in making the considerate gestures people will continue to associate with your business.

Promotional Follow-Up

Virtually the same rules apply here as for the follow-up after a media conference, outlined in Chapter Eleven. If the event concludes at a reasonable time, make telephone calls to the media immediately after it ends. The next day issue statements and photographs about the important aspects of your event. As with media conferences, promotional events can result in a ripple effect leading to subsequent coverage through talk shows and feature stories.

13

More Media Access: Public Service Messages

Radio and television stations reserve free broadcast time for those whose messages serve the community interests. Public-service announcements, free-speech messages, community calendars, and public-affairs programs provide free media exposure. Although these vehicles are most often used by nonprofit groups, they can also be a workable source of publicity for business owners who are promoting products.

By contributing community service through work done for a favorite charity, for example, you can attract media attention and build public support. In addition to the free time offered on the airwaves, qualified groups can use free space in periodicals.

To use public-service access effectively you must master the art of fulfilling established requirements. The essentials are sensitivity to time requirements, clarity of purpose, properly prepared materials, selection of appropriate stations, and polished presentations.

Each station offers some public access. Check with your local stations to determine specific policies about your use of free air time. A station usually will not deny access because you are controversial. However, you can be required to meet certain public-service guidelines.

Establishing Eligibility

To take advantage of community-service air time and print space, you or your group must be nonprofit or must offer genuine community service. Your group may be either civic or social, and the message should be directly related to the activities of the membership.

If you are a business owner and fail to meet these qualifications, you may be able to develop a community-service angle. Think of ways in which you or your organization can genuinely contribute to the community.

One example of a successful community-service angle is that used by a clinic, in offering limited free medical care to the unemployed. The staff

Date
Name of your organization
Street address
City, State, ZIP code
Name of Person Preparing Copy
Telephone number

Speaker:

MESSAGE TITLE

Your first paragraph clearly states the name of the speaker and the purpose of the message.

I am Maxine Wonderful Citizen. We members of the League for Senior Joggers urge you not to concrete over the jogging path through our district park.

Your second paragraph presents background information in support of your claim.

Recent medical reports indicate jogging on concrete is injurious to one's health. Reports by the Park and Recreation Commission conclude that destruction of the fauna and flora will alter the ecology of the park.

The third paragraph is a statement of your view of the issue.

The proposal to change our beautiful and natural grass path into a concrete-covered roadway is ludicrous. Frankly, we seniors count on our daily walks through the park to renew our bodies and our spirits. Concrete won't contribute to our health or to the health of the park system.

The fourth paragraph states what action is requested.

Please write or phone the mayor today to let him know you are against the concrete monster that threatens to cover us all.

FREE-SPEECH MESSAGE

also sponsored free monthly informational seminars on health care and distributed a community newsletter on health issues. By implementing these public-service projects, the clinic received consistent, widespread media coverage and a marked increase in paying patients.

Another example is a department store that opens its doors every Christmas to offer a five-minute toy grab—free—to underprivileged children. Other organizations get lots of ink and air time by giving summer jobs to teenagers. In addition to the good feelings that come from these meaningful contributions, businesses garner valuable free publicity. No matter what the nature of your business, you can develop a public-service angle.

Another approach for a profit-making business is to donate services or products to a nonprofit when it is sponsoring an event that will attract media coverage. For example, provide food to be sold at a handicapped children's decathlon, or contribute an item to an auction.

During the course of the publicity campaign, volunteer to appear on a community-service program. Discuss the necessity for local business owners to contribute community service. When media cameras and reporters turn out to cover the event, be certain that a large banner showing your company name is posted in a conspicuous position.

This kind of media access offers indirect rather than direct publicity for your service or product. Nonetheless, it supports your goal of getting your name before the public in a favorable light.

Make contributions to organizations whose images are in concert with your own: contributing to your community will serve both you and the recipient. Look realistically at your current time commitments to charities and the gifts you may already be making to community groups. How can these contributions serve you?

Where and When

In order to choose the proper presentation and vehicle for your community-service message, first outline your needs. Who are your potential customers? Who do you want to receive your message? What is it you plan to say? To whom do you want to talk? After deciding on audience makeup, select radio and TV stations that serve this audience. Public-service directors will gladly assist you by providing audience demographics.

Gaining access to community-service time on radio or television requires that you begin to plan well ahead. Although different stations have varying lead times, allow at least four weeks to get your message before the public. Check with the stations you designate for their specific time requirements.

Pinpointing just when your message will be heard or seen is difficult. The decision maker balances the immediacy of your message against the audience's scope of interest. Making a follow-up call about two weeks after mailing may facilitate placement.

How to Deliver Your Message

All stations and newspapers accept written announcements, and some radio stations accept air-quality prerecorded announcements. Your choice of message format should be dictated by your purpose. Often, but not always, public-service directors have facilities and resources available that they can provide free of charge to help you get your message across.

You must present materials for your public-service messages in a specific format. The following are format guidelines for different kinds of public-service access.

Free-Speech Messages. These are statements of personal opinion on matters of interest to the public at large. They may be the opinion of an individual or of a group representative, and usually the message expresses a plan for change or improvement in areas of community concern.

Sometimes these messages are controversial, although they are not allowed to attack the character or integrity of an individual. They may not slander another person or use obscenities. It is inappropriate to use these messages to address ballot issues.

Present your free-speech message on a single sheet of paper in the format shown on page 126. It should be typed, double spaced, and approximately 125 words long. Telephone the public-service director at the station you select and ask for the name of the person who should receive your message. Within five working days following your mailing, telephone the station to make certain your materials have been received.

If your message is selected for broadcast, practice reading it aloud into a tape recorder (for TV, stand in front of a mirror).

Public-Service Announcements. These are very brief, from ten to sixty seconds, and usually relate to the activities of a nonprofit, tax-exempt community group. Stations may air announcements several times, and they may find more on-air opportunities if you supply them with messages of varying lengths.

Public-service announcements may be prepared for broadcast in several ways. The station may provide you with a studio and professional assistance in recording your message. In this case, practice by reading into a tape recorder; be conversational and keep in mind that these words are meant for the ear. Long sentences or hard-to-pronounce words will trip you up.

Alternatively, the copy for your public-service announcement may be forwarded to the station announcer to read on the air. Another possibility is that you record your message elsewhere and forward the tape to the station. For the best quality, use only a professional studio. In any case, you must begin by writing to the public-service director.

Here is an estimate of the number of words needed for the various time slots:

10 seconds = 25 words
20 seconds = 40 words
30 seconds = 80 words
60 seconds = 160 words

When preparing copy for your public-service announcement, be sure to include answers to the following:

What is the action you want to announce?
Who is sponsoring the activity?
Where is it being held?
When is it being held?
Why is it being held?

Also include a brief statement of the group's purpose and a telephone number where the spokesperson can be reached.

If you are submitting copy for announcements of differing lengths, each should be typed on a separate page.

To prepare your public-service announcement, begin with a rough draft of your message. List the points you wish to make. Sentences should be brief and conversational. Important information, telephone numbers, and dates should be repeated. Read your copy aloud. Time it carefully. Eliminate rough spots and words that slow the flow of your copy.

When you have refined the copy so that it presents the information you want, put it on a standard sheet of white paper in the format shown on pages 130 and 131.

When you submit public-service announcements to a local television station, your chances for airing are improved if you present a visual that relates to your issue or organization. The most commonly used visual materials are 35mm slides, videotape, and, less often, film.

Check with your local stations for their requirements. Make every effort to meet these requirements rather than adhering to a general format that may not be appropriate.

The format for television public-service announcements is shown on page 132.

Date
Name of your organization
Street address
City, State, ZIP code
Name of person preparing copy
Telephone number

Speaker:

15-SECOND MESSAGE

Be accurate. Be brief. Repeat significant dates. Keep the sentences short. Triple space if possible. Make certain the copy is readable. Eliminate complex words and long sentences that stop the reading flow.

PUBLIC-SERVICE ANNOUNCEMENT FOR RADIO

Public-Service Programs. These are the early-Sunday-morning panels, Saturday-afternoon talk shows, and predawn debates that you no doubt have dialed past on your television set. Next time, stop; you will see that these shows are an abundant source of free publicity. What's more, appearances can catapult you to other, mainstream media opportunities.

Contrary to what you might believe, these shows are watched, listened to, and adored by large segments of the population you might want to reach. Local stations offer a wide variety of these public-service programs. They often discuss issues surrounding community problems and the concerns of various social, ethnic, and political groups. Interviews, panel discussions, and in-depth presentations of issues are the vogue for these shows. Study the issues and formats so that you are prepared to deliver an appropriate, professional presentation.

The procedure for approaching public-service talk shows is the same as that detailed earlier for approaching talk shows generally. Contact the TV station for the producer's name, or refer to the media directories listed in Chapter Seven. Send a media release to the show's producer

Date:
Name of your organization
Street address
City, State, ZIP code
Name of person preparing copy
Telephone number

Speaker:

30-SECOND MESSAGE

Help us save the park trails as you enjoy a delightful evening of fun and enter-tainment. Join singer-juggler Sandra Cane as she headlines the Senior Joggers' Fund-raiser on September 20, 1986, to benefit the Fund to Save Park Trails. Pro-ceeds will be used to halt city efforts to concrete the trails. Participants who donate $25 will enjoy a sumptuous dinner, music, and a dance contest. For tick-ets, contact your local TicketMaster outlet. That's September 20, 1986—a fun evening for the entire family.

PUBLIC-SERVICE ANNOUNCEMENT FOR RADIO

explaining the nature of your action or issue. Do your follow-up calling in the manner described in Chapter Eight. Place special emphasis on how your issue or action affects the community.

If you are representing a nonprofit organization, this process will be quite simple. If you are a businessperson looking for access, as always you must link your action or event to a community-service news peg.

Community Calendar Announcements. Special events may be listed free on radio, on television, and in newspapers. Examples of appropriate occasions are community theater productions, city ballet performances, art exhibits, and street fairs. Copy is limited to the bare-bones facts of what is happening:

Event
Group sponsoring event
Description of activity
Date, time, location
Purpose of event
Ticket information

Date:
Name of your organization
Street address
City, State, ZIP code
Name of person preparing copy
Telephone number

Speaker:

AIR DATES: BEFORE SEPTEMBER 20

30-SECOND ANNOUNCEMENT
television with graphic: slide

SLIDE IDENTIFICATION
Slide is of senior group walking along path to be covered with concrete by city.

STATION ANNOUNCER
Help us save the park trails as you enjoy a delightful evening of fun and entertainment. Join singer-juggler Sandra Cane as she headlines the Senior Joggers'
Fund-raiser on September 20, 1986, to benefit the Fund to Save Park Trails. Proceeds will be used to halt city efforts to concrete the trails. Participants who
donate $25 will enjoy a sumptuous dinner, music, and a dance contest. For tick-
ets, contact your local TicketMaster outlet. That's September 20, 1986—a fun
evening for the entire family.

PUBLIC-SERVICE ANNOUNCEMENT FOR TELEVISION

Submit your materials at least five weeks prior to the event. In some
areas the lead time is longer, so check with each media outlet.

Public-service access can yield a satisfying harvest of publicity and
can serve as a relatively simple introduction to dealing with the media. It
is a good arena in which to develop your media skills and professionalism.

PART FOUR

PR Power in Action: Specific Strategies

14

Promoting Your Medical Practice

If you are a physician with a rare specialty, a one-of-a-kind plastic surgeon in a posh neighborhood, a general practice physician in an isolated mountain town, or a doctor who can generate weight loss with magic shots, read no further. Simply describe your specialty (in lay language) in a handsomely turned out media-release package, distribute it to all the local media outlets, and prepare to be interviewed.

If, however, you are within the mainstream of medicine, you might consider delivering your service in a unique fashion, one that will attract and hold the attention of patients and titillate the minds of reporters and talk-show hosts.

Gone are the days when the town physician had patients waiting in line. Everyone knew Old Doc Jones because he had always healed their relatives and friends. Besides, Doc Jones was probably the only doctor in town. Patients had little or no choice in who would care for their runny noses or sprained ankles.

Today people have the privilege of shopping for doctors. Patients can afford to be fickle because there is another physician just around the corner. With the advent of neighborhood medical clinics and the expansion of group practices, some locations have an abundance of medical care.

The availability of these choices may work to the advantage of patients, but it has created a bit of a dilemma for physicians. They have to package and sell themselves. They can no longer wait for word of mouth to spread the message of their services.

Until recently most members of the medical profession frowned on using publicity as a way of attracting new patients. As competition has grown, however, so have physicians' aggressiveness in seeking new patients. Many physicians now use dignified public-relations campaigns to promote their businesses.

It is not uncommon to see physicians as regular guests on media talk shows. Many have sought professional training in emoting in front of the camera and even host their own talk shows. Others have secured regular segments within prime-time television or radio newscasts. They seek exposure on the airwaves and in ink because they realize publicity brings patients. The cold, hard reality is that few physicians, except the superstars of their fields, can afford to ignore the trend toward self-promotion.

For you who are still queasy about promoting yourself, the good news is that you can communicate the excellence of your service with dignity. Promotion needn't be crass campaigns that violate your medical or personal ethics. Promoting your service, if done properly, can enlighten the public about medical options in protecting good health and treating ailments.

Finding Your Niche

Any entrepreneur who begins a promotional campaign must first determine how he or she measures up to the competition. What is different about the level of quality you offer? What is it about your service that makes it more appealing? Is the location of your practice a real help to patients? Do your available hours make your services more convenient? Do you offer a wide range of quick medical services beneath one roof? Do you offer a baby-sitting service in a beautifully decorated room? Do you make home visits one day a week? What do you have that the other doctors in your neighborhood do not have?

Because the potential patient is not knowledgeable about the intricate details of practicing medicine, it is difficult to tout your surgical procedure over another's or to boast that your medical education and experience make you better qualified. Furthermore, the ethics within the field make it unlikely that you would choose to publicize your skills at performing face-lifts or tonsillectomies as being superior to those of your colleagues.

As with any service, what you are selling is satisfactory results. The more ways you find to satisfy your patients' needs while complying with and embracing the Hippocratic oath, the more patients you will have. Although you may not be able to compare publicly your expertise with that of others in your profession, you can emphasize the special ways in which you choose to deliver your service.

Who Are Your Patients?

Prepare a profile of your patients. Who are they? Where do they live? What is their level of income? What is their work schedule? When will they most likely need medical services? If your practice is in pediatrics or geriatrics, these are easy questions. But if your patients fall into some middle range, target a part of your community on which to focus your attention. For example, middle-income working families need a particular kind of service; wealthy pregnant women would find a different scale of service appealing. A patient profile will allow you to gain insight into ways of tailoring your services.

Two physicians in partnership found a way to boost their patient enrollment. They had purchased a freestanding medical-care center in a bedroom community adjacent to an industrial section just south of San Francisco. Although there were several similar care facilities nearby, they experienced a surge of patient enthusiasm for service during the early months of their practice when they spent considerable amounts of money on advertising. But even at its peak, the volume was not high enough to support the practice. The doctors felt they had the capacity to double their number of patients and still maintain quality service.

Having identified their target patient as coming from nearby young middle-income families and workers at the industrial center, the doctors decided to adjust their hours of service to the convenience of their patients. They shuddered at the prospect but nevertheless extended their hours into nights and weekends.

The unique hours were a focal point of their first media campaign. Media releases were sent to as many community bulletin boards as possible. The doctors stopped shuddering when remaining open Saturday morning, Sunday afternoon, and two nights a week brought a local television news camera and positive responses from an increasing flow of patients.

Getting Media Attention

A basic need of every physician hoping to promote a practice is a well-written biography. You also need a profile of your practice and services, with emphasis on your medical specialty (in language that's not too technical, please). Emphasize special aspects of your training or experience—for example, working with natives in the jungles of Borneo or rejuvenating malaria victims in India.

Create a medical-philosophy page in which you express your opinion on issues that will interest your existing and potential patients. You may decide to address provocative issues, such as organ transplants, life-support systems, and innovative ways of treating traditional ailments.

If you practice in a small town where there are few physicians, simply mail your media packet to the various print and electronic media and await requests for appearances. Metropolitan physicians need to incorporate their biographies and media releases into a larger plan.

Do not ignore an opportunity to research and write a special paper for a local medical convention on a highly controversial subject or one that contains long-awaited information. The convention's publicist might be sending out generic media releases, so have your staff distribute a release on your behalf. Include the specific time of your appearance and provocative tidbits from your paper. Keep in mind, however, that if you disclose too much, there is no need for a reporter to cover your appearance.

Another vehicle that will ensure you get some attention from the media is a book on a topic of broad public interest. Especially popular are books that inform the public about nontraditional health care choices—safe sex in the age of AIDS, the decision to choose the sex of one's child, or home health care for the ailing child. And of course, books on medical aids to retaining youth and beauty are always a hit. If your schedule does not permit the time to write it yourself, do what your colleagues are doing—find a ghost writer or coauthor.

You do not need to write a best-seller; the task is simply to have a book in hand. However, if the book is respected by your colleagues, utilized in the local university, and number two on the *New York Times* best-seller list, so much the better.

If you live in a community where there is no physician on the air with a local talk show, consider hosting one yourself. It is worth thousands of dollars of free advertising and will no doubt bring in patients. Besides, you just might have fun.

A local television cable station or mainstream station might be willing to help you learn the ropes and plan a show. It's to their advantage to have you present medical data that interests their audiences.

Consider, too, writing a column for a local newspaper, magazine, or even one of those shopping giveaways. Don't let lack of experience stop you. Write three columns on varying topics. Mail them to the newspaper editor, along with your credentials and an offer to contribute a regular column. If the first editor refuses, send your proposal to other papers in your area.

If you feel you are a terrible writer, there is another option: there are firms that write medical columns and sell them to physicians for printing under each physician's name. I suggest, however, that you take the time to write your own.

Rising Above Your Competition

Media folks find general practitioners and discussions of maintenance health care boring topics. Significant discoveries, issues, or events—these are hooks on which to hang media releases. In an urban community like San Francisco, there is an endless line of doctors always waiting to appear on early morning and noontime TV news or talk shows. But two unknown doctors found a hook and a way to get on the airwaves.

Combing through periodicals, they found several stories about unemployment in their community. They decided to donate one day a month to providing free medical care to unemployed persons who demonstrated a real need. The doctors invited other members of the community to donate medical supplies, doughnuts, coffee and tea, and other support services. Putting together this program allowed the doctors and their clinic's staff to make many contacts in the community. This not only reduced the costs of the program but also added substantially to their patient base.

Releases announcing the clinic's effort to help the unemployed were distributed to media outlets. It was immediately obvious that the medical giveaway and community effort struck the media's fancy. During that first month, three television news spots and a half-page profile in the local newspaper boosted the daily (paying) patient load. This patient increase leveled off after a period of six months, but the practice was then established. It continued service to the unemployed throughout the year-long PR campaign. The two doctors and their innovative program had garnered so much publicity that they received a letter from President Reagan congratulating them on their good work.

Another physician who was having trouble building a one-man practice used a simple, old-fashioned idea that worked like a charm. Amid the hustle and bustle of city life, this doctor began a family night. On one evening a week he held an open house for his patients and their families and friends. At first only immediate family and friends came, and then friends brought their friends, and then strangers came by to question the doctor about their problems.

The doctor also gave up his golf day and began home visits. There was a surcharge for his travel time, but the patients who used the service were overjoyed. The media got a kick out of his horse-and-buggy remedy. The doctor found he was benefiting as well. Soon he required an associate to handle the extra patient load.

Reaching into the Community

You cannot remain a stranger within a community and expect to build a large practice. In tandem with their promotional campaign and weekend hours, the two suburban San Francisco doctors mentioned earlier worked hard at building ties within the local community. They wrote letters to other doctors in the area announcing availability at odd hours and offering to serve their patients. On a warm Sunday afternoon they held an open house specifically geared to fellow physicians and their families.

Each of the physicians also joined the Kiwanis club, the local Chamber of Commerce, the school board, police and fire organizations, and other local charities and organizations. They scheduled their lunches so they could participate in gatherings within the business community, and they volunteered to speak before the PTA, high schools, and other community groups where potential patients might meet them and become comfortable with them.

The Chamber of Commerce provided the doctors with a list of community street fairs and special gatherings where they could set up temporary stations and offer free blood-pressure checks. At the same time, they initiated a series of free in-house seminars on topics chosen to appeal to their target patient: "Preventing Winter Colds"; "Filling the Family First-Aid Kit"; "Protecting Your Family's Good Health"; "When Your Child Swallows Poison"; "Welcoming the New Arrival to the Second Family"; "Sex in the 1980s." Seminar announcements were sent to community calendars in all media. Press releases were mailed to local talk shows offering the physicians to discuss the focus topic. Fliers were distributed throughout the neighborhood.

A number of seminar attendees remarked that they had seen the clinic on television or had read about it in newspaper articles. The two promotion elements had worked in tandem. Because people were familiar with the names and faces of the doctors, they chose to attend the seminar.

The seminars brought in a sizable share of new clients and were considered a contribution to the community. They also provided continuing opportunities for media coverage.

Simultaneously, another phase of the PR campaign was beginning to pay off. The clinic had sent the customary letters to company medical directors in the area describing the nature of the clinic's care-giving and emphasizing efficient service and immediate attention to on-the-job injuries. This led to a contract to provide medical care for employees of an industrial company.

The physicians offered to conduct brown bag question-and-answer sessions at businesses and factories during lunch hours. They had a polished and professional presentation that they held to forty-five minutes. Some of those appearances were preceded by media releases and public-service announcements to newspaper, television, and radio community calendars. It all paid off in still more patients.

Limits on Advice

Regardless of your skill, there is always a need to be careful about spur-of-the-moment diagnosis and the possibility of malpractice. During personal or media appearances, do not get caught in the malpractice trap of giving specific medical advice without having examined the patient. All advice should be preceded by words such as "You should see your doctor" and followed by words such as "It appears that..." or "Sometimes it is possible that..." It is best to give generic advice about hypothetical symptoms; in all public circumstances, provide general information and steer clear of direct diagnosis or the slightest suggestion of possible specific pharmaceutical cures.

A Direct Link to Patients

A well-written, visually appealing brochure is another method of attracting new patients. It need not be elaborate and glossy but should be a compendium of words and pictures that warms the heart. It becomes the part of you that patients can take home. It is also a publicity piece that patients can pass on to their friends and coworkers.

One of the most effective promotional tools is a newsletter. It gives you the opportunity to provide valuable medical information to patients and potential patients. Newsletters can also be distributed to local businesses and given to audiences when you speak. Newsletters, like brochures, provide a way for you to describe yourself and explain your practice, allowing people to become familiar with your office and services. It should include information (emergency medical-help numbers) and offers of free services (blood-pressure or diabetes checks). Newsletters should also include articles, announcements of your next seminar topic, and descriptions of other educational services, such as a lending library of relevant medical videos.

A newsletter sent regularly by mail, with pictures of the exterior of your office and of you and your staff interacting with patients, makes a wonderful messenger. Patients can browse through your newsletter at their leisure, becoming familiar with you and your office. This familiarity can eventually bring them across your threshold.

Although this list of tasks necessary to promote your service may seem exhausting now, you'll probably find that you can handle these duties joyously when you see a great rise in patients and income. As time passes, promoting yourself will become second nature; with the support of staff, PR will require even less of your time.

15

Promoting Your Legal Practice

With today's scramble for clients law firms no longer question whether to use promotional campaigns but ask instead how to do so with the dignity that preserves the honored traditions of the profession. Much of the previous chapter on medical public relations also applies to the legal profession. This chapter will focus on the elements of legal public relations campaigns that differ from medical PR.

Deciding Which Cases to Promote

By virtue of the processes involved–documents filed are public records, arguments and facts are presented in an open courtroom–exercising legal PR power is a complex and sensitive task. It is not always possible for you to control what the media will discover and report. A reporter leafing through public records may expose a portion of a case you have represented that you do *not* want exposed. Exercising your legal PR power may sometimes entail managing what is to be revealed to the media as well as attracting media interest to the newsworthy aspects of your case.

When considering what case you will choose to promote, carefully examine all the elements. Is this a case in which you and your client can withstand close scrutiny without fear of disquieting revelations? Is the judge in this case overly sensitive to publicity? Is there now or has there been a gag order issued in this case? Is your client articulate? Does your client portray his or her plight in a way that will help or hinder the overall goal of your litigation? And, most importantly, how does your client feel about publicity?

The cases that most readily lend themselves to promotion are personal injury suits. All the elements are present for good publicity: you have the aggrieved victim, the family of the victim–all presenting opportunities for public suffering and accusations–and the villain, huffing and puffing in defense of his or her actions. Standing by the side of the aggrieved victim is the attorney on a white horse, ready to defend and protect the client. Who could ask for more? We all like stories with clearly delineated characters. So do the media.

One major consideration in choosing which cases you will publicize is which kind of client you wish to represent in the future. The case you spotlight in the news will attract more cases just like it: if you really want to represent only million-dollar personal-injury clients, don't promote the public-interest freebie you are spearheading. Otherwise, following the publication or airing of news of your freebie, you will be pursued by other public-interest-freebie clients.

Defining Your PR Goals

Why do you want publicity and what do you expect to accomplish by getting it? Is it to get more clients? To bring about some desired effect in a case? To establish your public image as a base for running for public office? Do you anticipate that publicizing this case could affect its direction? For example, if you are filing suit following an airplane crash or other large disaster, you can use media exposure to attract additional plaintiffs.

If your publicity goal in a given case is to enhance your own public image and practice, then the focus of your press release and your press conference would be different. You would begin by announcing your decision to take on a tobacco company or a drug manufacturer and explain why you will succeed although other attorneys have failed. With the emphasis on yourself, you would stage press conferences only in your office. Your clients would not be present, or if present, they would remain silent, allowing you to speak on their behalf.

If, on the other hand, your interest in publicity focuses on the plight of your client and winning the case, the major portion of your release would explain the client's dilemma. Perhaps the last sentence would refer to your participation in the case: "Mrs. Johnson is represented by attorney Deborah Smith."

A decision about your PR focus at the outset becomes a guideline for how you will conduct the campaign.

The Legal Media Release

The legal media release follows the same format as demonstrated in Chapter Five. Begin with an explosive title: ATTORNEY DEBORAH SMITH SUES CIGARETTE COMPANY FOR FIVE MILLION DOLLARS; CRASH VICTIM SUES AIRLINE FOR TEN MILLION; A BILLION-DOLLAR KISS—FEMALE DEPUTY SUES SHERIFF FOR MANHANDLING.

Your media release should be written to plug into the headline while focusing on the aspect of the story you wish to emphasize. It should follow a journalistic style and read like the well-written news story you want it to become. The least important information goes at the bottom of the page. Remember to keep the tone brief and provocative.

Of course, if the act that spawned the lawsuit has been the subject of current news stories, you have an even greater chance of sparking widespread publicity.

You must have a well-written biography and office profile to accompany the media release, especially if the goal is to enhance a personal image. Some attorneys lean toward a slick media packet: a glossy folder with gold-embossed letters and a hair-spray picture on the front. Avoid this image! It can result in a harsh response from the media. Reporters become irritated if they suspect an attorney is pushing too hard to get publicity through a client's case.

Even the flamboyant types don't overplay their media packets with glitter and gloss. They may show up for the press conference driving a gold-dusted Rolls Royce and wearing an Armani suit, but the media release that preceded them was written on stately gray paper in a matching folder with dark blue lettering.

An exception to the conservative approach would be an announcement of a special holiday party in your office, a celebration of your twenty-fifth anniversary in business, or a billion-dollar win in a personal injury case.

The Pitfalls of Publicity

One unfortunate consequence of a press release can be to point the media toward a too-talkative client. Cases have been toppled by loose-mouthed clients or chatty secretaries anxious to please reporters on the phone; stories in print that reveal your legal strategy prematurely or divulge a valued tidbit of information about your client (unknown to the opposing side) can be "bad news." All attorneys know the value of keeping detailed information about cases close to their vests. Consequently, an important prerequisite to the legal media release is the attorney's control over all elements of the case.

Designate a spokesperson for the media and have everyone else involved take a vow of silence. Ask yourself if the individual you choose as spokesperson portrays the image you wish to convey. (If you are the spokesperson, ask yourself the same question.) All inquiries are referred to the chosen spokesperson. Clarify with the spokesperson the message you wish to convey during a media conference or interview and prepare a written list of hypothetical questions and answers. You may even want to note within the release that "Attorney Deborah Smith or Mrs. Susan Jones will be available for questions."

Preparation is the key to ensuring successful interaction with the media and the publicity you desire.

Issuing a Legal Media Release

Timing is especially important in mailing legal media releases. Do not mail your release or contact the media in any way before your documents have been filed and all parties have been served. Not waiting is unprofessional behavior and will no doubt result in inappropriate publicity, especially if the uninformed respondent glowers at the reporter and asks, "What lawsuit?"

Developing material for media releases during the early stages of a case is fairly simple. Plaintiffs are asserting their undeserved pain; defendants are declaring their innocence. This kind of provocative public bickering can generate great coverage, the kind that always brings attorneys more clients. Media types love blood and guts because it is a guaranteed winner with their audiences.

Issuing media releases later in the case—before the announcement of the judge's ruling on a motion, before the resolution of a settlement conference, or while the jury is out—can be very risky. What if the other side wins? They may bask in the glory generated by the media release you mailed. It is better not to announce events that may quickly turn against you.

There are times when you want to avoid media interviews and not send out releases. During these times you batten down the legal hatches. If a reporter wants to talk, there's no need to be rude. A refusal with respect and polite candor is always best: "I'm just not in a position to talk about this right now" or "As soon as I have something I can talk about I'll be glad to get in touch" or "Although I appreciate your interest, it's not a good time for my client to speak with you." Assistants and secretaries saying that you are unavailable will work for a time, but such behavior can alienate the reporters you might need to count on for coverage at some later date. Treat media representatives the way you wish to be treated. Acknowledge calls at all times. Be clear and fair in your refusal to answer their questions.

Except in rare cases, it is inappropriate to promise that you or your client will give an exclusive interview. Offering a news scoop to one reporter to the exclusion of all others is a dangerous game, one in which you are likely to be the loser. If you make such commitments, be prepared to be snubbed by the reporters whom you left out.

Should you develop a social relationship with one reporter, keep your professional life separate. Whispered answers to "off the record" questions are to be avoided without exception. Remember Watergate! In the presence of a reporter, do not let words cross your lips about your case, your client, or any issue of substance if you would not be comfortable seeing those words attributed to you in a news story.

Choosing Media Outlets

Send releases to the news assignment desks of mainstream media and, in addition, to the legal writers at each station or periodical. These people have a special interest in the law that can be stimulated by your point of view, but be aware of what they may have written regarding the opposing side.

You can compile a special legal media list by simply calling local media, including the legal newspapers, and asking for the names of their legal writers. Update these lists frequently because there is often quick reporter turnover.

Depending on the nature of the story, also send media releases to city-beat reporters and to special-interest reporters. If you are involved in a case dealing with an environmental issue, send releases to the assignment desk, the legal reporter, and the environment reporter all at the same newspaper. This kind of cross-mailing is necessary in all radio, TV, and periodical outlets.

Reporters in one department often do not know what other departments are doing. Do not count on sending one release and having people kindly pass it along to whomever it belongs. They seldom have the time or the inclination. It is better to send too many releases than to risk being overlooked. Additionally, you will increase the possibility of coverage if during the morning decision conference more than one person is aware of your story and thinks it is a good idea.

When mailing to television or radio stations, remember to target public-service-interview and general talk-show outlets. Examples are local shows with the same format as "Good Morning America." These shows provide a showcase for you to express your views and give audiences an opportunity to learn who you are and what you offer.

To make a good talk-show guest, develop points of view relative to general legal issues of public concern. Prepare a clear and brief presentation of issues involving the case you have been called upon to discuss. Although you may not want to go on at length about a specific case, you can present a well-thought-out view of general issues involving cases similar to the one you are litigating. However, the caution flag goes up here because your opponent or the judge—or even your client—might misinterpret something you say, or some reporter might take what you say, apply it to the current case, and print it.

Following Up on Your Mailing

Five to seven days after mailing your media release start your follow-up calls. These calls should be made in accordance with the general instructions in Chapter Eight.

You, the attorney, should not make the calls. However, the person chosen to follow up should have some legal savvy and should have read the brief and other documents relating to the case. Although the follow-up caller should be instructed not to discuss the substance of the case, legal writers will ask questions about its mechanics. The follow-up caller should have knowledge of the facts: in which county and department documents were filed, what motions are before the judge, who the judge is, where the courtroom is, and so on. The more the follow-up caller understands the law the more valuable he or she will be to the attorney.

Beware! Little telephone leaks from your follow-up calls can muddy the waters. There must be no hint of surprise announcements or intimate tidbits about the case or the client's shortcomings. No doubt you've seen those pieces on television: the attorney is taken by surprise when he or she discovers that, even before a motion is made in court, the follow-up caller had inadvertently revealed the substance of the motion to the media and it had been broadcast or printed.

Keep in mind that the legal writer is probably talking to the opposing side as well. Sometimes the media will try to inveigle a reply from you by releasing provocative information. Avoid any tendency to play this game.

Attorney on the Media Hot Seat

Review information in Chapter Ten about interview techniques. An attorney giving an interview should remember that the reporter does not necessarily understand the legal process even though he or she uses legal jargon. Do not become embroiled in webs of legalese, explaining the technical reasons why you have chosen to make certain moves. Explanations should be concise and simple enough to be understood by any high school graduate, unless you are speaking specifically to a journal that caters to other legal professionals.

Remember to frame your answers in an interesting manner, juxtaposing the issues of disagreement. A boring, flat answer, one with no fire or intrigue, will get you a dud of a story with no prospect for a return visit by the reporter. If you wonder what constitutes this proper framing, observe attorneys who are regularly interviewed in the media. What is it about their presentations that makes them desirable?

In legal matters especially it's important to remember that the interviewer is not your friend. To reveal future legal strategies, to give inside information on other parties to the case, or to hypothesize about possible rulings can result in disaster. Negative words about the judge should never cross your lips. What you say can be embellished or misinterpreted and printed or aired. You will have a limited chance of rebuttal. Avoid the anguish of explaining your media statement to an angry judge—on or off the record—by not saying it in the first place.

Beyond these special interview considerations, you must do your homework and be knowledgeable about the facts of the case. As the interview proceeds, keep your goal in mind. What are you trying to imprint upon the minds of those who will see or hear your interview? What is your goal in terms of the outcome of the case? Spewing a broad range of information allows the reporter to choose what will be printed or broadcast—choices that could be quite different from those you would have made.

One attorney speaking to a room full of reporters—lights on, cameras rolling, pens scribbling—made his first mistake in mispronouncing the plaintiff's (his client's) name. His second error was to identify the defendant, a man, as a woman. From there it went downhill as the media courted his ignorance. With chest high, he proceeded to pontificate about various aspects of the suit, including the location of the incident and the extent of the damages. The next day, newspaper stories and news clips paraded his ineptness before a wide audience. Avoid this embarrassment.

The Legal Media Conference and Its Aftermath

The fact that you have won a verdict in one personal injury case is not of particular interest to the rest of the world unless the person is well known, the incident has generated significant publicity in the past, or the verdict sets a precedent that opens doors for similar lawsuits. If the consequences of your case will affect the public, however, you have a reason to notify the news media that is even more compelling. Calling a media conference is clearly appropriate if a class-action suit has been settled and members of the public who have been harmed by a particular product should file a claim. If the amount your client has been awarded is significantly high or if there is something unique about the award, this is also legitimate news copy.

As usual, take care in your decision to call a media conference. One attorney called a media conference to announce his lawsuit against a major car manufacturer on behalf of two severely injured parties. He had videos that showed commercials of the car moving at high speed to support his claim that a defective braking system was at fault. All was going well until a reporter read from the police report that each of the plaintiffs had a blood alcohol content high enough for them to be considered legally drunk.

Inevitably, even if you are meticulous about legal public relations, there comes a time when the outcome of a case is not what you had expected: a client talks out of turn or the jury votes the "wrong" way. Responding to media questions in pain or in anger does not help your image. You can show disappointment and a wide range of emotions without becoming weepy or hitting a reporter over the head. Lashing out before a camera will always be remembered by the audience and played up by the media. Strength of character is what appeals to people seeking an attorney. A swift, brief, and dignified response is always desirable.

Following any kind of media blitz about you or your client, prepare to respond to an increased number of phone calls. Have a polite, sympathetic person with some legal savvy answer your telephones during and after your appearance. No matter the time of day or night, someone should be available to comfort callers and to direct them toward your services. Easing fears and directing callers toward immediate relief is the approach that will attract new clients.

Brochures

A brochure that explains the nature of your service, how you deal with clients, and your philosophical view of the law can be very helpful. It is an immediately available tool for explaining your practice to potential clients who might visit your office. It is an effective handout wherever you speak. It can also be used in direct mail efforts to introduce yourself to the neighborhood and in your media packets when you are mailing information to talk-show producers and editors.

More Ways to Promote Your Legal Practice

Write a Book. Take a controversial stand on a legal issue or explain the law to the folks down home. We are not talking about a best-seller or a book that merits a chair at a prestigious university, but simply a book that will inform the public and serve as a vehicle for getting you air time on talk shows or ink in the press.

Write a Legal Column. Submit a proposal to your local newspaper, whether daily, weekly, or giveaway. If you can't write it, you can use companies that specialize in writing the copy; you put your name on it. Of course it is preferable to write your own.

Host a Media Talk Show. Analyze your local radio and television stations. Do they have a regular attorney who speaks on legal issues and informs audiences about how to protect their legal rights? If not, draw up a proposal, attach your biography, and mail it to the station director. Consider getting professional coaching to sharpen your on-air talent, if you feel you need it.

Hold Seminars. Create a series of public seminars on issues that relate to your field of law. Each seminar provides an occasion for informing media outlets and community-service calendars about the seminar topic—and your credentials. Consider topics related to your specialty that also appeal to the public: "The Divorcing Male—How to Protect Your Assets"; "Women and Community Property Rights"; "Protecting Your Small Business"; "Insurance, IRAs, and Your Will"; "When Your Teenager Hits Someone while Driving Your Car."

Write Newsletters. Newsletters on legal issues are popular these days. Especially appealing to the reading public are newsletters that give information about personal liabilities within the home, small business liability, and how to protect personal rights. Topics for exploration could include parking tickets, wills, rights of visitation by divorced fathers, liability when your dog bites the mailman, eviction, or tenant and landlord issues.

Other Sources of Clients

Everywhere you go there are opportunities to promote yourself (see Chapter Four). Whether joining the local chamber of commerce, volunteering your services for a charity, or jogging along a popular path, you'll encounter people who get excited and want to ask questions when you introduce yourself as an attorney. Personal promotion is a key element in public relations for any service.

16

Promoting Your Book

If you're willing to exercise your PR power, publishing your own book can be fun and even more profitable than if it is produced by a major publisher. When you self-publish, your earnings are directly related to how much you're willing to promote your book. It takes persistent effort to send out media packets, make follow-up calls, give interviews, and create new reasons for the reporters and talk-show hosts to include you in still another round of publicity. This chapter describes promotion for self-published books, but the advice is equally useful for authors who want to supplement the efforts of their commercial publishers or for anyone who wants to understand the publicity process for publishers.

There are many inspiring stories of self-publishers who generated best-sellers and incredible financial returns. *A Whack on the Side of the Head* by Dr. Roger Von Oech is one such success story. Published in the author's garage in 1983, this book is still on bookshelves around the world, having sold more than seven hundred thousand copies. After a brief publicity campaign, Von Oech sold so many books that a major publisher offered him handsome payment to take it over. Even though the book is now published by that publisher, the author has not stopped promoting his book. His persistent efforts at publicizing himself and his book have kept it alive.

To sell their books continuously, even authors whose books are purchased by major publishers find it necessary to conduct public relations campaigns. Major publishers subscribe to the "flash-in-the-pan" effect: if your book is a potential best-seller, at first they pour heaps of cash into publicizing it; but if the public does not respond immediately they quickly abandon your book. It is the authors who have the courage of their convictions, who patiently and meticulously contact media outlets, that are gratified by the results.

For the self-publisher, promoting a book is rather like gold mining: if you're willing to roll up your sleeves, be patient, and keep digging, there is a much better chance that you'll find gold. It's your task to inspire the media: A book is born! A book is born! Greet it with a rousing welcome!

Targeting Your Readership

Your first task is to know your customer. Who will find value in what you have written? Is yours a professional book with a small and very specialized target audience, or is the book of general interest, one that will appeal to a wide spectrum of readers? The answer to this question sets the tone for your promotional campaign.

If your book is of special interest to people within a certain field, collect lists of all the organizations, groups, businesses, and persons in the field who might want to purchase the book or have you speak about your book before their groups. Also compile a list of the names and addresses of specialized journals, bulletins, and periodicals concerned with the topic of your book. Clip ads placed by related organizations in magazines and newspapers. Note television shows that present guests who speak on your topic. And, of course, keep a file of friends, acquaintances, and even relatives who will be interested in purchasing and recommending your book. Then be prepared to expand and modify your approach.

For example, one person wrote a book on color charts, believing her book to be important to the fashion industry. She modified her promotional and marketing campaigns, however, when her biggest market turned out to be members of the awning manufacturing industry, painters, contractors, and interior decorators.

The Brochure: A Handy Messenger

A brochure is a useful tool for promoting your book to the media during the early stages of the book's development. Create a brochure that conveys the message of your book and tells, in a well-written paragraph, why your book is important to today's reader.

Include a clever but brief biography, explaining the compelling reason why you wrote the book. Emphasize your special knowledge of the field about which you are writing. For example, you are a long-distance runner writing about the trials of training, or a stepmother writing about overcoming the objections of her stepchildren. List special honors, awards, and accomplishments that add credibility to your approach.

If you already have endorsements by well-known people within the field about which you are writing, quote a sentence or two of the best comments. If you already have a positive review from a respectable periodical, of course include it.

The brochure can be sent with review copies of the book, invitations to book parties, and direct-mail order forms. Because it will be seen as a measure of the quality of the book, this is no time to cut corners. If you can't design and print a handsome brochure, have a professional do it for you.

Reviews

There are two kinds of reviews: prepublication reviews directed to the book trade and publication-date reviews directed to the buying public. Prepublication reviews are primarily for the benefit of bookstores and libraries that will stock your book. They depend on these recommendations and summaries to make their buying decisions. Some newspaper and magazine book-review editors also refer to these prepublication reviews to determine which books should get attention in their columns.

Reviews for readers at publication time are an important tool in promoting your book to the public. After you have received some favorable reviews you can expect interviews, feature stories, and other attention from the media. Reviews are most helpful if they appear close to the book's publication date. Keep in mind that you want publicity to appear in tandem with your book distribution. It does you no good to have people say nice things about your book when there is no book yet available to purchase.

Promoting Your Book: Prepublication

Promoting your book at the earliest possible stage can result in obtaining increased orders from distributors. Even before the book has come off the press, send bound galleys (proofs of book pages without illustrations and with a plain, glued-on cover) to appropriate book trade periodicals for prepublication review.

Accompany your galleys with a brochure (if you have it), a press release, and a letter explaining who you are and the nature of your book. Your media release and all your materials should be presented on your visually appealing letterhead. Include endorsements from recognized experts and your professional qualifications; these will give the book credibility. Include in the press release the retail price, ISBN (International Standard Book Number), Library of Congress Cataloging-in-Publication data, publication date, and how the book can be ordered by bookstores and wholesalers.

At least ninety days before your release date the bound galleys should arrive at prepublication review magazines. The key magazine is *Publishers Weekly* (249 W. 17th Street, New York, NY 10011). This magazine, which almost never reviews books after their publication, is the bible of the book trade. A favorable review in *Publishers Weekly* can net you thousands of orders from booksellers. *Kirkus* (200 Park Avenue South, New

York, NY 10003) is another important trade magazine that reviews forthcoming books.

Library Journal (at the same address as *Publishers Weekly*) and *Booklist* (American Library Association, 50 E. Huron Street, Chicago, IL 60611) cover the library markets; *School Library Journal* (at the same address as *Publishers Weekly*) and *Choice* (100 Riverside Center, Middleton, CT 06457) review for school libraries. They reach thousands of librarians throughout the country who might order your book because of favorable reviews.

Also consider sending bound galleys far in advance to the *New York Times* (229 W. 43rd Street, New York, NY 10036) for the Sunday *Book Review* and the daily "Book Critic."

Never underestimate the importance of favorable prepublication reviews in these periodicals. These reviews can mean national attention and distribution for your book.

Promoting Your Book: Postpublication

Your next priority is to distribute media releases to the magazines that review books on or after publication. Spend a morning in the library acquainting yourself with all the magazines you would like to review your book. Refer to the following reference books to find postpublication media outlets:

Literary Market Place (a complete directory of all stages in book publishing, including periodicals interested in newly published books)

Gale Directory of Publications (newspapers and magazines, organized geographically)

Urich's International Periodicals Directory (special periodicals)

Bacon's Publicity Checker (separate volumes for newspapers, magazines, and trade journals)

Editor & Publisher International Yearbook (daily and weekly newspapers)

Working Press of the Nation (five volumes on all media)

and three trade association directories:

Encyclopedia of Associations

National Trade

Professional Associations Directory

Coordinating Promotion with Distribution. It is your responsibility to undertake promotional campaigns in cities where your book has been distributed. Begin your press campaign where you live. One advantage of starting your media campaign close to home is that it allows you to stick to a small promotional budget. Another advantage is the native son or daughter factor. The media usually have some investment in local pride; being able to tell them you are a local person who made good is an advantage. Additionally, you are likely to have some contacts at home and, therefore, more immediate access to reporters, editors, and producers.

After you have garnered a few reviews and interviews, make copies (preferably printed instead of photocopied) and add them to your media packet for the second round of mailing: the nearest out-of-town points to which your book has been distributed. Send media packets and make the usual follow-up calls to achieve your goal of scheduling as many appearances and interviews as possible. No doubt you have seen authors come into your town and hit the media like a shotgun burst, appearing on every television station, conversing on all the radio shows, and hitting the newspapers. That is your goal—to hit the media with a blast.

At the same time, begin to blanket the national media with packets and systematically to hit the towns where your book is selling.

Media Packet Materials. Your media packet should include a media release (the publication announcement of the book), an information sheet explaining the scope and content of the book, a brief biography of yourself, your picture, and a copy of your book. For packets going to media out of your area include an itinerary of your promotional tour, highlighting the date you expect to be in each recipient's city.

Your media release reflects the excitement you feel about the publication of your book. It conveys to producers and reporters the book's value to the public. Written in the inverted pyramid format discussed in Chapter Five, it announces the publication of your book and gives a *brief* and intriguing summary. Write the summary to convey the kind of enthusiasm that will seduce even the most disinterested person into reading your book.

Because book editors receive perhaps hundreds of releases each day, the first line of your release should be a killer. The first paragraph should rivet reviewers' attention to what you have written. Your media release must provoke reviewers enough that they open your book and read it. Why should book reviewers, reporters, or editors want to read your book if even your media release is boring?

If possible, connect your book topic to some event, activity, or issue currently in the news. Highlight that you are presenting long-awaited new information. Emphasize what is different about your book.

Your photograph should be professionally done. It is from this photograph that television producers decide whether you will be appealing to their audiences, or radio and newspaper editors will decide whether you are interesting enough copy to keep the attention of their listeners and readers. Newspapers and magazines may also publish your photo with their reviews.

Although it is advisable that you play it straight and use a good likeness of yourself, depending on the nature of the book you might be able to have fun with a photograph. For example, for a fun book with the theme of helping the reader to let go of all appropriate notions of one's self to stimulate creative thinking and actions, the author practiced what he preached: he sent media packets with a picture of himself dressed in a Superman costume, taking advantage of the fact that he resembled both actors who played Superman in the movies. Editors and producers were delighted that this creative genius with a doctorate degree would behave in that manner. The photo earned him many spots on the air and pictures in print.

The photograph you include in your media kit should be in concert with the image your book portrays.

Using Excerpts as Publicity

If your book is a do-it-yourself primer or a celebrity biography, or if it can be excerpted for a wide audience, you may be able to convince a local newspaper or magazine to accept a chapter. Write a query letter to appropriate periodicals, summarizing the book's content and apprising them of your credentials. Specify a chapter or two that would be perfect, or offer to write a condensation. Keep in mind the lead times, which can be several months.

Selling excerpts or condensations—called serial sales—can also yield considerable income, but here we are concerned with only the promotional value. The excerpt or article can generate buying interest in your book either before or after it is published. However, the ideal time for the excerpt to appear is as close as possible to the book's publication date.

Stirring Media Interest

A book signing can become a full-fledged media event. It is an important link in your publicity campaign. Some bookstores, believing that your book will be a hit or wanting to support certain kinds of books or local authors, will stage book-signing parties for you. Keep abreast of their plans for your event. Make sure that you are comfortable with those plans and that the invitation list is comprehensive.

Signings and sales can also take place outside the bookstore. Some authors hire actors, stuntpersons, or cartoon characters to attract patrons to a party. Others serve hot finger-food on a street corner while a white-gloved pianist plays away, or they hire a Chinese dragon and gong to lead people to their book party. In a small town, the music, balloon, or dragon might make a good visual media story, especially if the book has special interest to the residents.

Another plan is to connect your book signing to an event already generating publicity, like a downtown street fair. Or attach your book signing to a charity, perhaps donating the proceeds from the first sales. Make certain the publicist for this group agrees with your purpose and will support you in making it the kind of event that attracts media attention.

Of course, the kind of event you plan should be in keeping with the subject matter of the book and your image as its author. You would not hire a clown for a book on a serious topic. But remember that there are fifty thousand books published a year in the United States—almost a thousand a week—and you should not be shy about attracting some attention.

17

Promoting Your Nonprofit Organization

In this time of dwindling philanthropic funds and exploding causes, donors will support the nonprofit that best communicates its good deeds to the public. The intrinsic value of a specific service, no matter how wonderful, may go unnoticed and unfunded if the nonprofit cannot make known its uniquely indispensable community service.

No matter what your cause or who you serve, one sure-fire way of promoting your organization is to solicit a high-profile, glitzy board of directors. These folks are not necessarily the working board but rather the rich and famous, with recognizable names and well-established reputations, who attract public attention and spotlight the importance of your cause.

To overlook this key factor in building public recognition is to court disaster. Yes, you may have a board of working Trojans, ready to sacrifice everything for your cause, but the board members must be able to command the attention of the media and have their phone calls returned by wealthy influential businesspeople.

In addition, you need board members who can connect directly with the people who allocate foundation funds. Decisions regarding who gets the big bucks are often made on golf courses, in locker rooms, or during lunch at the club. If you have no pipeline to these inner sanctums, your nonprofit may suffer.

Building a Workable Base for Community Support

From the outset, assign board members sets of tasks. Worker bees and queen bees should be quite clear about their respective roles, responsibilities, and methods for accountability. If indeed you have high-profile persons on board, no doubt they will tell their friends about you and attract others who can aid your cause. With their permission, seize every opportunity for using their names to the organization's advantage—on fundraising invitations and in media releases, for example. Then, when a media opportunity presents itself, send a high-profile board member along with a staff member or officer who has a thorough working knowledge of the projects and programs.

High-profile members might also get a kick out of using their homes to host the media conference when you announce your fund drive to house the homeless or find adopting families for physically challenged children.

You must also determine what board members expect in return for their services and whether those expectations are appropriate. No one likes to be taken advantage of. We all like to feel that we, too, are getting something out of the venture. Even well-known people are willing to exchange the use of their names for the prestige of being associated with a cause that gives service to the community and the fun of being a media darling, along the way being honored with plaques and certificates.

The Preparation that Pays

You and your board should attend a seminar in the art of fund-raising. Although many novices are well meaning in their efforts, often they don't really know what to ask for or, if they do, whom to ask for it.

One group of new board members visited a millionaire and asked for $50,000 for their worthwhile charity, which he gave them. The next day they heard that on the same day they had visited the man he had donated $500,000 to a local charity. Board members called to ask why he had given them only $50,00. "I gave you what you asked for," he replied. "You didn't ask for $500,000."

A four- to six-hour seminar can substantially raise your yearly fund-raising results by helping you refine your fund-raising process and target your donors.

Meeting the Media

After you refine your fund-raising process, focus your primary efforts on one major fund-raising event each year. That event, if handled properly, can promote your public profile and generate year-round goodwill and donations.

Auctions are a popular fund-raising event. Board members gather items donated by community businesses and invite the public to bid on them. Because auctions have become commonplace, the standard approach is not as productive as it once was. Therefore, if you decide to hold an auction, consider having a specialized event that will garner extra media attention. For example, auction celebrity items. This allows the media to preview the rock star's tennis shoes or the Shakespearean

CHARITIES UNLIMITED
PRESENTS:
A Non-event
July 15
On behalf of The Children's Orphanage

For Immediate Release

For more information contact:
Beautraux Do-Good
(415) 555-5555

PUTTIN' ON THE RITZ—AT HOME

"Put your feet up—stay home, vegetate in front of the television. Don't bother getting your favorite sequined gown out of storage or pressing your tux—forget about those shoes that pinch. Relax and enjoy our NON-EVENT. You're being fêted to an evening of pleasurable excitement right in your home, without noise, rich food, excessive alcohol, or exhaustive nice-making with people you don't especially like to be with."

These are words from the invitation of Charities Unlimited's sparkling NON-EVENT. Socialite board members Ella Fitz Randolph and Sarah Van Frotz will not be attending the NON-EVENT, which would have been held at the St. Martin Hotel, but will instead schedule a family massage hour for the evening. They've asked their friends to schedule a quiet evening at the pool table, in front of the television, or stationed at chess boards on the evening of July 15.

The Bees Wax Orchestra, which would have donated its services, is instead contributing cash. Business owners who might have donated services or products are instead sending checks.

Invitation recipients are asked to donate the $150 per person or $2,500 per table they might otherwise spend for an evening of gala frolic.

Charities Unlimited officials report profits from this NON-EVENT will be used to fund a new wing of the orphanage.

MEDIA RELEASE

actor's tux. It also provides an opportunity for one of the stars who has donated items to be present, drawing even more media attention.

You have probably been overwhelmed with fund-raising ideas from cake bakes to footraces; one organization had a clever idea—it sponsored a nonevent. It sent members, supporters, potentially interested strangers, and the media brightly colored packets naming a specific date on which they would be allowed *not* to attend an event if they contributed a hefty amount of money. One reason the organization received lots of media attention was a clever invitation. It listed tasks associated with staging a huge event, and in accordance with the amount of the donation, it released each recipient from participating in the dreary work details. Invitations sent to community dignitaries noted that they would have been invited to speak or officiate had there been an event. In addition, special nonevent notices were prepared for newspaper calendars and radio public-service announcements.

The idea charmed everyone. It was especially dear to those people who suffer from nonprofit-fund-raising-event overload. Of course the media were intrigued by the idea and interviewed people on what the event might have been like had it taken place. Reporters flocked to the organization to cover its good deeds and to applaud the wise fund-raising tactic.

The media release on page 160 was used, in keeping with the spirit of the non-event.

Whether you use this or any other idea for a fund-raiser, the task is the same—to choose an issue or idea that attracts media interest as well as the public so you get your idea across to as many people as possible.

Opportunities for Media Coverage

Significant developments within the field in which your nonprofit operates, the appointment of a new director with especially glowing qualifications, being awarded a large grant—these are all occasions when you might want to issue a media release. Be cautious about issuing releases too frequently, especially when there is little substance or no visuals that might interest the electronic media. Consider the needs of the media when you target your media releases. For example, specialty magazines might be interested in your activity, but it might not be suitable for television or radio.

If you take the time to become familiar with the needs of the media, your efforts will be rewarded with coverage when you need it. Radio and television stations in your area might even offer courses to nonprofits on use of the media. It is well worth your while to invest the time and energy in attending such courses.

To ensure a functioning conduit from your nonprofit to the public, establish a relationship with the public service or community service departments of your local media outlets. Because you are a nonprofit, the media are especially agreeable to airing or printing your announcements. Follow the media's requested format and make sure your announcements reach the media before their deadlines. (Chapter Thirteen discusses public-service announcements, an important vehicle for nonprofits.) The competition is stiff for this kind of exposure, so the slicker your idea or presentation (without being gaudy or pretentious) the greater the probability that you will get the exposure you wish.

Nonprofits are moving toward more sophisticated promotions, which presents you with a reason to be creative in your approach. Because your goal is to sell the idea of supporting your cause, you must reflect the committed passion you feel for the cause. Half-hearted approaches will simply be ignored. The dedicated soldiers who march forth with banner high in the name of their causes will garner the most media attention and hence the public support needed to survive.

18

Quick Inspirations:
PR Ideas for 100 Businesses

This section is designed to give you an instant dose of inspiration. The ideas are intended to jump-start your thinking cap and get you started promoting yourself. Think creatively. List all the crazy things, the absolutely outrageous things you would never do for publicity, and then do the ones you can put into action without great expense.

However, to litter the desks of editors and producers with badly written, badly researched junk will not serve your cause. Any suggestion here assumes that you will do your homework and that your intentions are to provide the best possible service or product. Shoddy offerings are always discovered; those that you publicize are discovered even faster.

Competition for placement on the airwaves or in print is considerable. Those who pay meticulous attention to detail and present their ideas with integrity and a sincere desire to serve will most likely be chosen. It's up to you to preserve the privilege of public access to the airwaves and print.

One general tip should be kept in mind: if you can't sell it, give it away. Donating services or products to charity often commands attention and starts an energy flow that results in increased business activity.

Good luck!

Accessories Store
• Donate your services and lend accessories to models in a local charity auction or fashion show. Organize free seminars demonstrating the use of accessories for the budget-minded or the wealthy woman. Provide accessories to the men officiating at a local golf tournament. Organize an all-male fashion show—for women only.

Accountant
• Offer your services at an odd time. Beginning at Thanksgiving offer stress-free tax preparation during evenings and Saturdays. Host seminars on tax preparation in July.

- Claim that your office is a quiet port in the tax-season storm. Provide soft music and snacks. Offer baby-sitting services.

Acupressure Therapist
- Write an article for a local magazine. Join a local fair—offer half-priced but limited services to first-time users.

Advertising and Marketing Firm
- Offer to provide free advertising and marketing consultation for a high-profile charity (limited to the hours of service you can afford to give away).

Answering Service
- Focus on services not ordinarily offered. Call yourself an electronic secretary. Offer regular clients the opportunity to be reminded of birthdays and anniversaries through your reminder service.
- Tailor your features to the needs of a specific business population—small businesses or construction businesses.

Antique Store
- Conduct informational seminars on antiques. Invite a new catering business to serve one item of food from the era being discussed. Offer to appraise antiques free one day each month.
- Donate a special item to a charity auction.
- Write a column on antiques for the local Sunday newspaper magazine, spinning wild and wonderful tales about odd pieces of furniture.

Apartment Rental Agency
- Offer seminars in tenant and landlord rights.
- Find a moving company that will join with you in an advertising venture. Hold a drawing for a free move by the company.

Appliance Sales
- Hold a seminar on appliance repair for women only. Organize a fair with outdated appliances, complete with a history of their development. Award a door prize of a free appliance to the patron holding a lucky number.

Architect
- Conduct free seminars on low-cost additions or alterations to family homes. Issue media releases and public-service announcements.

Art Gallery

- Offer on-site art classes in the techniques of the Old Masters. Offer art appreciation for the unenlightened. Nurture and develop your customers' tastes for the kinds of art you sell.
- Print a newsletter filled with information and ideas about artists and their work. Host an auction to benefit a local charity. (See media release "Pre-Opera Festivities," page 166.)

Artist

- Hold a showing in your work space. Show actual works in progress.
- Offer to teach tiny tots, senior citizens, or the handicapped the art form you practice; provide lessons at a reduced rate or free of cost.

Astrologist

- Predict the winners in a local election and have your predictions officially sealed. Have your favorite auction solicit donations based on your percentage of correct predictions.

Athletic Club

- Sponsor an unusual athletic event—tennis for grandmothers over fifty, race walking for grandfathers over seventy, wheelchair basketball, or swimming meets for eight-year-olds.
- Organize a series of seminars on self-esteem, weight reduction, relationships—whatever your competitor has overlooked.

Auto Dealer

- Join MADD—Mothers Against Drunk Driving—especially if you are male.
- Sponsor a television talk show or a late-night movie with inexpensive ads. Be certain they will allow you to join the host live on the set when you wish.
- Create a theme and have salespeople dress accordingly.

Baker

- One day each quarter bake old-fashioned bread and sell it at a 1910 price.
- Deliver your leftover baked goods to the homeless, to elderly shut-ins, to the underprivileged.
- Develop a special bread or dessert uniquely your own.

THE METERON GALLERY TEN DOWNING ROAD BRANCHWORTH, TEXAS

For Immediate Release

For more information
contact: Sally Smith
(817) 777-7777

PRE-OPERA FESTIVITIES

Members of the Branchworth Dames are gathering for cocktails and chatter at the Meteron Gallery before the premiere performance of *Aida,* on Thursday evening, October 30. The reception, which will begin at 5:30 p.m., will highlight the Dames' fund-raising activities on behalf of the Children's Hospital.

The Meteron Gallery has donated "A Scattered Dream," the much-talked-about sculpture by Brian Chattington, as the featured item during the silent auction. Proceeds from the auction will benefit the children's cancer ward.

Established in 1987, the special ward has been praised by experts around the country for its room-in facility for families and for its successful treatment of youngsters under five years old.

Gallery owner Bret Meteron has announced a series of pre-opera events that will benefit several charities for children throughout the city. The Gallery, which opened in 1980, features objets d'art ranging from the classics by grand masters to recent works by local artists.

Provisions have been made for the media.

RSVP Sally Smith, 777-7777.

MEDIA RELEASE

Beauty Salon
- Create a package deal: customers receive a permanent and an overnight stay in a local hotel.
- Make house calls.

Bed-and-Breakfast Accommodations
- Offer a romantic weekend for couples married more than five years who have children. You provide the babysitting.
- Court local organizations and corporations to have their soul-searching, nurturing weekends at your place. Make them offers they can't refuse. The follow-up business will more than pay for providing reduced rates.

Billing Service
- Do family seminars on budgeting, bill paying, and reapplying for credit.
- Present small-business seminars on making collections.

Boat-Rental Service
- Offer newlyweds or those celebrating their tenth anniversary a free moonlight boat rental. Provide a violinist and special food donated by a local gourmet deli (that also needs promotion).

Bookstore
- Hire animated performers in costume to draw Saturday crowds.
- Focus on making your bookstore the expert seller of a specific field of literature: Italian history, romance novels, long-forgotten biographies, show-biz books.
- Promote a week in which you will appraise (for free) antique books your customers find in attics.

Boutique for Clothing
- Offer a special demonstration of packing—how to travel for three weeks with one suitcase.
- If you are a woman's personal-wear boutique, offer a holiday evening for men who need help in choosing just the right item for their ladies' Christmas or Valentine gifts.
- Hold a seminar that advises women on choosing clothing for their men, whether at holiday time or on a regular basis. The media go wild over such male-female intrigues.

Business Manager
- Create a business incubator—give a free consultation once a month for four hours at a popular restaurant or location.

- Write a column for a business magazine or business section of a local newspaper.

Career Consultant

(This is a big topic for radio talk shows.)
- Attend all Career Day fairs. Coin a phrase that emphasizes the unique aspect of your service: "Before midlife, we give you new life as we help you find the career of your choice."

Carpenter

- Offer seasonal specials: for spring, closet shelves; for winter, fireplace-face construction; for summer, deck construction.
- Offer carpentry services that allow the homeowner to participate and learn the trade at the same time. Structure your price levels to include two or three levels of service, which allow price breaks for those who wish to contribute their own sweat.
- Offer a package to your clients that provides detailed follow-up on any repair or building you do—six months later.
- Offer to demonstrate tips on household repairs for morning television shows aimed at homemakers.

Carpet and Rug Dealer

- Offer your potential clients information about the relationship between allergies and dirty carpets and drapes. Invite a noted allergist to hold a seminar on the subject.

Caterer

- Focus on promoting one unique aspect of your offering: ethnic meals, cookies that don't melt in little kids' hands, quick-fix carry-out meals.
- Donate your services to a major event, with the provision that you can post signs and hand out cards.
- Offer to transform ordinary food into intriguing animal or plant shapes. Become famous for your tasty sculptures.
- Offer specials: those who choose your catering service will get free music for the evening. Combine forces with a good musician who is trying to make a name as well.

Coffee Shop

- Become famous for a special brew.
- Once a month on Thursdays offer an old-fashioned cup of coffee for an old-fashioned price—ten cents.

Computer Consultant

- Present free miniseminar classes that meet the needs of specific groups. Examples: "Computers for the Elderly," "Toddlers and the MAC," "Word Processing for Bunglers," "Entering the Computer Age without Pain," "Computer Wizardry for Idiots." After you draw your crowd, offer your expanded learning programs and whatever other services you wish.

Consultant

- No matter what your consulting service is, writing a column, distributing your own newsletter, and offering to speak before a local group will pay off.
- Donate your services to a charity auction.

Contractor

- Take color photos of the houses you have built, or have them videotaped. Offer your clients the privilege of constructing the house of their dreams (in full color) on a computer, so they can see what it will look like.

Convalescent Hospital

- Offer in-house musical shows donated by local talent. Enlist the help of a local celebrity or would-be celebrity. Request that other community businesspeople contribute services or products to this special once-a-month event. Garner the help of a local radio station to broadcast direct from your hospital.
- Offer in-house classes on popular topics: "Relationships," "Aging with Grace and Spunk," "Romance for Seniors," or "Life after Heart Attack."

Cruise-ship Owners

- Do unusual theme cruises: a romantic evening for pregnant women, or family cruise for couples married more than thirty years. Create some incredible winter cruise for the hardy.
- Offer discounts to special groups at special times, such as June graduates or September brides.

Dating Service

- Offer a special service to those reentering the dating market who are fifty and older.
- Sponsor a larger-persons dating group package.

Delicatessen

- Develop a sandwich or salad dressing and name it after a famous person in your city. Have that person christen the item during a naming ceremony.
- Offer at a special low price one sandwich with the kinds of ingredients that will attract the media—like a no-cholesterol, all-vegetable filling with an odd, no-wheat bread.

Designer (Clothing)

- Offer to have your fashions included in auctions given by highly regarded charities. Usually the women officiating at these charities are the women you'll want to buy your designs.

Dressmaker

- Offer sewing classes or private sewing lessons. Create situations in which you assist people to make their own garments.

Dry Cleaners

- Offer specials. Attach discount coupons to each bill.
- Combine services: offer a dry-cleaning service with a shoe-repair service, or a laundry service with a convenience store for quick shopping.

Employment Service

- Write a book or pamphlet on how to take the pain out of job hunting. Devise a formula that specifies steps anyone can use.
- Conduct special seminars on employment for older job hunters. Offer seminars on job alternatives: finding a job-sharing situation or working part-time.
- Create a unique class of specialists: grandmothers as baby-sitters, or retired teachers as tutors.

Environmental Consultant

(Lucky you—any person having to do with maintaining the integrity of the environment or resurrecting it has an open season with the media.)

- Make friends with your local TV weatherperson and provide a unique interpretation or explanation of an environmental hazard or the effort to prevent the hazard.
- Teach the kids on your block to clean a field, guide the Boy Scouts to clean a beach front, help neighbors rid themselves of toxic cleaning chemicals, point out businesses in your immediate area that are dumping toxic materials down the drain.

Event-Planning Service

- Donate your services on behalf of a popular charity that caters to your potential clients. Demonstrate your skills by planning the most extraordinary event ever. Be wild, be daring. Don't be boring and the media will surely follow.

Executive-Recruiting Service

- Invite all the executives you've placed in the past to return for an open house. As your triumph, point to the longevity of your placements on the job, the most unique placement, or the extraordinary number you've placed.
- Write a book on executive recruiting, emphasizing what is different about your methods. Give seminars.

Fabric Shop

- Invite volunteers to stitch blankets for the homeless. Hold classes; teach children under twelve to sew and complete garments.
- One day only, offer an old-fashioned fabric at the price your mother used to pay.

Ferryboat Service

- Offer unusual entertainment or informative classes at certain times of the day: "How to Make Certain the House You Are Buying Is Right for You," "Fireproofing Your Home," "How to Reduce Taxes."
- Offer a contest to find the most romantic couple. Have spouses or partners nominate their choices and tell why. Offer a moonlight cruise with strolling musicians, awarding a six-month pass to the most romantic couple.

Financial Planner

- Offer free seminars using an unusual hook: "Defending a Woman's Fortune against Her Mate's Greed during Divorce." To garner media interest, pick the kinds of financial solutions that meet the needs of a broad spectrum of people.
- Write a series of articles for your local newspaper entitled "Money, the Third Partner in Every Marriage." Describe the specific steps and decisions that lead "Joe" from an ordinary income to a financially comfortable position.

Fireplace Sales or Service

- Prepare a demonstration of proper fireplace procedure when there is a Christmas tree in the room. Provide information about the danger of not cleaning one's fireplace. Properly placed public-service announcements and free demonstrations will result in widespread public interest. The winter holiday-season months are especially appropriate for promoting this field.

Fishing-Party Boat

- Allow partners or dates to come along free of charge. Offer your boat to a local charity, like Parents without Partners, for special holiday fun at a reduced rate.

Floor Covering/Refinishing Service

- Carpet the town square during a holiday celebration. On your local cable television station, offer advice about do-it-yourself floor finishing.
- Organize a fair presenting the floors of the future or one featuring the floors of your dreams.
- Become involved in decorator showcases (usually on behalf of non-profits). You are likely to be included in a media release, and if your contribution is significantly creative, you could garner lots of attention from reporters and cameras.

Florist

- Donate your services in flower arranging for the mayor's swearing-in, significant weddings, and community events that cater to your kinds of clients.
- Sponsor an exotic-flower fair. A simple, inexpensive setting for the presentation will do. Your media release should be full of little-known information about exotic plants. Focus on their extraordinary beauty and unique properties.

Formal-Wear Rental Service

- Hold a fashion show featuring high school seniors. The door prize is free rental of a tux for the postgraduation party.

Fund-raising Organizations

- Be creative about your approach for raising funds for a high-profile organization. For example, Junior League wives can auction off their husbands to benefit their favorite cause.
- Establish yourself as an expert on trends in fund-raising and issue media releases. Give specific data as they relate to your community. Offer a creative solution uniquely geared to interest your community.

Furniture Sales

- Become a furniture expert. Develop a wealth of information about the special care needed for different kinds of furniture, about the kinds of furniture people in your area are buying—and why. Write columns, hold seminars.
- Sponsor a sidewalk furniture fair in which you display new furniture and miraculously refurbish old furniture.

Garage/Parking Service

- Offer a Saturday afternoon guitarist to soothe shoppers' brows.
- Offer a valet washing service and once a month give away a free wash.
- Conduct a yearly drawing for free parking on behalf of charity.

Gift Shop

- Offer a shopping service that has a unique feature; for example, delivery within an hour (for an extra-rush fee, of course). Call your service The Wife Saver. Write a media release for the local social column and refer to a socially prominent husband whose wife was soothed by your last-minute delivery.

Graphic Designer

- Offer your services in the auction of a charitable organization. Your full listing in the catalog is a big sales booster.
- Decorate the outside of your place of business with extraordinary graphics.

Grocer

- Sponsor a Shop-A-Ree on behalf of your favorite high-profile charity. The winner grabs as many items as possible from your shelves within a brief allotted time. Television cameras always follow such events.
- Create an old-fashioned shopping day, offering ten items at the same price your grandmother paid.

Hardware Store

- Fix-it sessions for women are always sure winners. Set up a situation in which you have a group of women build a tool shed or a playhouse in a backyard. Send out a media release asking just how equal women have become—can they really be Ms. Fix-its?

Health Club

- Grandmothers in leotards, stretching toward the sky, or grandfathers chinning up—opportunities abound for creative visuals. Create aerobics for seniors, exercises for the handicapped, and a family plan for fitness. Creating special plans that give reduced rates to various groups usually attracts customers. (Health clubs require continuous special promotion.)

Hobby Shop

- Open the shop one evening each week and create a hobby club. Award prizes for the most complex model completed.
- Describe your shop as a vehicle for keeping family members communicating with each other. You are offering the alternative to couch-potato land.

Housecleaning Service

- Are you a dirtbuster, a lifestyle facilitator, or a personal systems manager? Whatever you decide to call yourself, make it interesting. Describe your service as specializing in serving single working mothers, single working fathers, or busy working singles.

Ice-Cream Parlor

- Go for the obvious: an old-fashioned day in which servers dress in costume and sell ice cream for the price paid during the 1950s or 1960s or, if you're brave, the 1920s or 1930s.

Interior Designer

- Offer clients a mini-decor package in which you simply visit their homes and arrange the furniture and objets d'art they already have. Give this process a name particular to you.
- Interior decorating seminars are always popular; that's why you will need a unique focus to muster media attention. For example, conduct your seminar in the local secondhand store, showing clients how to incorporate items there into their homes to create an effective look while on a tight budget.

Investigator

- Invent your unique personal speciality, like the Sherlock Bones who finds lost dogs.
- Are you a husband finder or a wife follower? Convey your specialty to the media in a way that intrigues.

Jeweler

- Search for the unusual—the extraordinary but affordable.
- Join forces with an already highly visible fashion designer and sponsor an event (whether or not on behalf of charity). Display the work (on

consignment) of an unknown designer who makes outrageous one-of-a-kind pieces.

Judo Instructor
- Teach self-defense classes to a specific group: women who live alone, seniors, teenage girls, bus drivers who work night shifts.
- Write a pamphlet on self-defense specifically aimed at an unusual segment of the population.

Knitting Shop
- On-site knitting classes are the best way to attract clients. Knit an entire wardrobe from lingerie through winter coat and have a fashion show on behalf of charity.

Lamp Store
- Display a lamp from another era or a recent copy of a lamp that exists in a queen's palace.
- Pick a historical figure and re-create part of his or her room in a corner of your shop, emphasizing the lighting. Invite a local antique furniture dealer to join in your display. Send releases to newspaper calendars, giving a specific date for the showing.

Laundromat
- Offer a large-screen TV for your waiting customers and feature instructional programs and courses. Announce your schedule in local newspaper calendar sections. (If your budget doesn't permit investment in either the course videos or the television, find companies that will agree to lease you such equipment and material; offer to let them run a trailer telling viewers who they are and where their products are available.)
- Combine your space with other businesses or promotional programs; for example, income tax preparers, fitness centers, supermarkets, barber shops.

Limousine Service
- Add an outrageous feature to your limousine. Provide clients with the option of a massage while in transit.
- Offer your vehicle's services at auction when the charity and potential audience include people who can afford your service.

Lingerie Shop
- Provide lingerie fashion shows targeting different groups: sexy lingerie for seniors, for larger women, or for the housewife over fifty who wants

to keep "him" interested. Ask a psychologist to join you for a seminar on "Sex and the Older Woman," or whatever topic you feel will titillate your clients.

Locksmith

- People always want information that will enable them to make their surroundings more secure. Target a specific audience and compile information that will serve them: how to enhance the effectiveness of a back-door lock or window lock, or effective lock alarm systems for a low budget.
- Provide information on how burglary statistics differ in your community and how most burglars enter homes.

Lumber Company

- Combine forces with a carpenter who is expert at home repair and home building; display work in progress one or two Saturdays a month. (Television stations often look for easy stories on the weekends, ones that are close by and will appeal to folks at home.) Send out a media release announcing the special focus of your event.

Mailing Service

- Offer a discount to folks who mail their holiday packages thirty days prior to the actual holiday. Offer other advantages to people who utilize your service at odd times when your shop is usually empty.
- Adjunct services—laundromat, video store—will make your business more visible, especially if you keep their longer hours instead of the Post Office's schedule.

Manicurist

- Target a segment of the population with an interesting offer: seniors who come in between 11 a.m. and 3 p.m. get reduced rates and a bingo game. Perhaps you have two rooms: one for those who want manicures and one for those who want to socialize. Of course the winner of the bingo game gets a free pedicure.

Massage Therapist

- Be truthful in promoting your skills: if they are limited to providing a soothing back rub and stress reduction, so be it. Offer clients a compilation of massage therapies, soothing music, and self-esteem tapes, allowing them to relax for a longer time than the typical session. Create a service that reaches far beyond your competition. Promote it by joining forces with a psychologist who is a stress expert. Offer your package at a Junior League or other such charitable auction whose patrons can well afford the appropriate fee.

Motel

- Family weekends are especially promotable because middle-income families are looking for recreation. Include amenities like on-site seminars in family relations or how to help Junior make better grades. Lessons in swimming, pottery making, and gourmet cooking sweeten the deal. Call your offer The Family Saver.

Mover, Home or Office

- Develop special techniques for safely moving objets d'art or pianos or pets. Is there something special about your moving team—as with the Mother Truckers (women movers) or Starving Students or the former drug addicts who feature both their work and their recovery? Does your crew have special brawn and equipment that allows them to move with particular speed and safety?

Musical Performer

- Perform for nonprofit events.
- Offer to entertain folks at the local senior citizens' home or give lessons to those out of the mainstream.

Nightclub

- Form a jazz-, rock-, or Dixieland-appreciation club. Members receive special rates for evenings of entertainment as well as the privilege of hobnobbing with performing artists.

Office-Products Store

- Provide seminars on setting up and operating offices. Discuss furniture configuration and equipment placement; bring in an efficiency expert who can talk about the best use of time in an office setting.

Optician

- Separate yourself from the pack by devising an innovative adjunct service: pick up and deliver, or provide a free, full-service checkup for any customer who develops a problem.
- Provide information and a seminar on proper eyeglass measurement and its relationship to the comfortable use of glasses or contact lenses.
- Donate services to a local nonprofit, the homeless, the unemployed, the underprivileged.

Painter, Exterior/Interior

- Reduce the fee for your services in exchange for your client allowing you to post a sign identifying you as the painter.
- Put together a pamphlet on how to preserve painted surfaces, how to choose paint that does not offend the respiratory system, or the connection between color and mood.

Party Giver

- Become a member of civic groups likely to throw community parties. Board service often leads you to the kinds of people who can afford what you are offering. If you can't become visible otherwise, offer to organize a huge event that benefits your favorite charity.
- Write a pamphlet or book on effective party hostessing, on how the ordinary can give extraordinary parties, on how the average apartment dweller can give an interesting and well-planned party in a small space.

Pet Groomer

- Offer tips to pet owners about specific problems they may encounter, such as how the pet owner could make the trip to the pet groomer more comfortable. What is it that you offer that is especially appealing to pets during this stressful time?
- Write an informational pamphlet that helps pet owners select the right pet groomer. What should pet owners look for to be certain the groomer provides the kind of care they desire for their pets?

Pharmacy

- Inform the public about the variations among similar prescription or nonprescription drugs. What about generic drugs: Is it true that some are less potent and less effective than name-brand drugs? Is it true that many people pay high prices for name-brand drugs when they could use the generic brand equally well? Write a pamphlet or hold seminars on shopping for the drug that is best. Select a special area, such as geriatrics or infant prescriptions.
- Plan one day a month when one item everybody needs goes on sale for the price paid in the 1950s. Have your salespeople wear the costumes and play the music of the 1950s in the store. An old-fashioned soda fountain would add an attention-getting touch, if it is appropriate for your store.

Photographer, Portrait

- Put a splashy photo on your business card, one that could hardly be ignored.

- Produce giant images of city dignitaries. Volunteer these photos for display in the windows of or inside a downtown department store to celebrate a special occasion.
- Volunteer your services as part of a package to be auctioned off at a nonprofit event.

Piano Sales

- Place a piano in the center of a shopping mall (noting the name of your shop on an elegant sign) and provide a pianist to serenade passersby.
- Pick an unlikely place to provide music, a place where you would not be intrusive and would soothe weary shoppers, workers, and sightseers.
- Donate free lessons to a specific category of the population: seniors on low incomes, underprivileged youngsters, destitute single parents, or the physically challenged.

Picture Framer

- Offer hands-on framing sessions during one evening a month. Free of cost, offer all comers the opportunity to learn the art of picture framing.
- Appraise old picture frames found in attic trunks.
- Write a pamphlet about how picture frames should fit into the decor of a room. Intersperse rare facts about obscure frame styles and their historic significance.

Podiatrist

- Offer yourself as an expert on footwear to preserve the integrity of the feet, or on footwear for the overweight, the elderly, or the physically challenged. This kind of information interests producers of early-morning magazine shows that feature information about family health.

Psychologist

- Write a "pop psych" book, coining a new term for an old neurosis.
- Choose a holiday, such as Christmas or Chanukah, when some people are likely to be depressed. Offer an open phone line to your community for specific hours and answer callers' questions. Announce your gift with a media release to newspaper calendars and news talk shows.
- Seminars, newsletters, and speeches before community organizations are three vital vehicles for attracting clients.

Real-Estate Sales, Residential

- Prepare a newsletter for middle-income families on creative financing and locations that might be affordable.

- If you specialize in high-priced homes, become the amenities queen or king of your area. Pick up your potential clients in a limo with an outrageous interior. Have a secretary in tow in case they need to dictate a business note; offer a gourmet breakfast with orange juice and special-blend coffee.

Restaurant
- Offer special prices to designated groups of people at special hours.
- Have unserved food left after 10 p.m. delivered to the homeless.
- Serve seniors a meal as they make crafts as presents for the underprivileged. (See media release "Betty's Senior Sit-In," page 181.)

River-Rafting Trips
- Provide instruction for a unique segment of the population, such as physically challenged children or seniors. (Investigate which of these special groups is the least costly in terms of your insurance.)
- Donate a trip at auction for the nonprofit that includes on its board, or within the organization, the kinds of people who are your potential customers.

School, Private
- Offer a series of free or low-cost seminars that will be of interest to any parent: "Turning Your Child into an Intellectual," "Preparing Your Child to Face the Job Market," "Accelerating Your Child's Education," "Helping Your Child Learn a Second Language."
- Prepare a pamphlet, or ask the principal or a teacher to write a newspaper column.
- Select board members with a high profile and impeccable social connections.

Secretarial Service
- Emphasize some aspect of your work that sets you apart. Are you the secretary on call, available night or day? Are you willing to work Saturdays, Sunday afternoons, or in the wee hours of the morning? Do you deliver? What adjunct services do you offer that your competitors do not?
- To celebrate National Secretaries Day, hoist a huge balloon with your picture and business name on it.
- Form a professional group with your local competitors to discuss triumphs and concerns. Because it's your idea, elect yourself president.
- Write a column for the general public on a topic relative to your

BETTY'S BISTRO   100 LARKENVAR   TUNNIS, ARIZONA

For Immediate Release

For more information
contact: Betty Coleman
(602) 777-7777

BETTY'S SENIOR SIT-IN

Betty's Bistro is sponsoring a Senior Sit-In on December 8, 1990, all day long. Seniors will gather at the restaurant on Monday to complete craft projects, which will be donated to the underprivileged as Christmas presents.

Quilting, doll sewing, ornament making, cake baking, cooking, dressmaking—all the projects Santa supervises—will be taking place. Rumor has it that the jolly old gent may even stop by to check on the seniors.

Betty is donating a hot lunch, including her famous Chicken Royal, for Santa's helpers.

Betty Coleman opened the restaurant twenty years ago. It has become famous for chicken dishes under 500 calories. Her recipes have appeared in *Home Magazine* and in her local cooking column in the *Tunnis Gazette*.

Local churches are donating materials for the toys and transportation to the Armory, where toys will be distributed. Anyone is welcome to join the day-long marathon. The only requirement is that you be 65 or older and have a project that is kid-worthy.

Betty's Bistro plans to make this Senior Sit-In an annual event.

MEDIA RELEASE

business and offer it to your local newspaper: "How Husbands Can Become Good Secretaries in the Home-Business Setting."

Travel Agency
- Provide seasonal updates for the media, in advance of the season, on the safest, least expensive, and most pleasurable places to travel.
- Become aware of which radio talk-show hosts and television magazine shows carry stories on travel. Peg your offer to appeal to their needs.

Upholsterer
- Offer specials that rejuvenate very old but intriguing furniture. Offer a free or half-price upholstery job to the person who brings in the oldest piece to be covered.
- Compile data on the history of furniture pieces that relate to your community and write a column, preferably in the shoppers' paper that needs copy and is read by people who would want your services.
- Give seminars on the art of upholstery repairs.

Video Store
- If your space is big enough and you have access to a large screen, offer a community movie night open to the public—by reservation, of course. (Because it's free you can probably get the listing and the name of your store in your local newspaper calendar.)
- Devise special themes, like a romance evening, lovers-of-Elvis evening, or an evening for those who adore Roy Rogers and Dale Evans, and offer refreshments as well as discounts.
- Offer information on movie memorabilia or current Hollywood gossip in a column or to a radio or television magazine show. (See "Hearts and Flowers," page 183).

Wardrobe Consultant
- Offer a miniconsultation service: advise customers how to make the best of the wardrobe they already have. Call it Your Closet Shopper and charge a low fee, so potential clients can get a taste of what you do.
- Hold seminars for a reasonable fee. Offer free seminars to local companies and corporations.
- Specialize in a specific group: larger women, teenagers, pregnant women, women executives.

Weight-Reduction Consultant
- Pick five high-profile people in your community. Offer them free diet instruction if they will be spokespersons for you.

THE FAXON VIDEO STORE   2204 LEXINGTON DRIVE   ANYWHERE, USA
What: In Celebration of Romance
Where: The Faxon Video Store
When: July 12, 9:00 a.m.to 9:00 p.m.

For Immediate Release

For more information
contact: Julie Faxon
(201) 777-7777

HEARTS AND FLOWERS AND KISSES AT THE FAXON VIDEO STORE

Many of the customers going into the Faxon Video Store on July 12 will be gazing into each other's eyes, holding hands, or walking arm in arm. On that date Lloyd Faxon, the owner, is giving all couples engaged during the month of July and those who celebrate their wedding anniversaries in July a discount on video rentals and sales. The July lovebirds will get half off any video rental or sale for the next six months and an opportunity to win a VCR.

Faxon has for three years been the sponsor of the Romance Movie Club. The shop features a wide selection of romantic movies in its comprehensive library of current titles. On the evening of July 12 local psychologist Martin Brockman will give a two-hour talk at the video store on "How to Put Romance Back into Your Life." The lecture, which begins at 7:00 p.m., is free to the public.

Lloyd Faxon and his wife, Julie, married twenty years, say they started the club because they feel with today's "fast-lane" lifestyle, couples seldom take the time to be romantic. "By encouraging romance we hope couples will focus on the real joy of taking time to be loving to each other."

MEDIA RELEASE

- Focus on the unique aspects of your service: perhaps the availability of fashion consulting for larger people.

Yoga Instructor

- Offer yoga to the physically challenged, senior citizens, or another unique segment of the population.
- Magazine talk shows will be delighted if you demonstrate that what you offer is not for contortionists or those endowed with extraordinarily supple bodies.

PART FIVE `

Evaluating Your PR Plans

19

Hiring an Outside Publicist

If business booms so much you don't have time to do your own publicity campaign, or if from the beginning you decide to put your efforts into another aspect of your business, you will need someone else to do your publicity. This chapter will tell you what you can and can't expect from an outside publicist.

The publicist's job is to help you identify a unique element within your business that sets you apart from competitors, and to assist you in formulating an image that reflects the value of your product or service. Even if you expect to hire the genius of the century, it is wise for you to have analyzed these issues yourself and to have some idea about how you wish to be seen and appreciated by the public. It would be a mistake to throw yourself on the mercy of a publicist, expecting that person to transport you to PR heaven. The process should be a working partnership with balanced participation by both partners.

It is the task of the publicist to translate the value and image of your business into a context and language that is appealing to the media. The publicist should be aware of topics currently favored by electronic or print outlets in the target geographic areas and should have contacts with key people in the media, especially decision makers who will be persuaded to cover your story.

A skilled publicist is able to position your story with the appropriate media so you receive specific opportunities for exposure to your potential customers. This implies that you contribute advice on this positioning, because you are the more knowledgeable about who your customers are and where they are most likely to be found.

Media releases, posters, and brochures created by the publicist on your behalf should be read and approved by you before they are sent out. Retain your right (in writing) to alter these materials if you so desire.

Certainly you should hire a publicist on whose expertise you can rely. If there is a question about how to handle aspects of the campaign, you should be able to trust his or her opinion and its basis in professional experience.

Having decided on a public-relations strategy, the publicist presents you with ideas and options you may not have considered and contributes the fresh ideas that will enhance your PR campaign. The publicist then creates written materials that reflect the image you want presented to the public. These materials are usually presented in a brochure (handed directly to your potential clients), direct mailing pieces (cards, posters, and handouts), and media releases.

The publicist will follow up the media mailing with telephone calls to pitch your story to decision makers and to schedule your appearances. A good publicist should have an aggressive plan for following up on the initial mailing; the success of a promotional campaign usually depends not on the glamorous names on your media list but on the doggedness of the publicist's follow-through.

Measuring the Dollar Value of Public-Relations Services

What would you pay for a three-by-five-inch ad in your local newspaper? What is the cost of a one-minute spot of advertising on local television? If a publicist gets you that amount of exposure without your paying for direct advertising, that is one measure of the dollar value of the publicist's services to you. Furthermore, research shows that readers give more credence to articles than to ads. An article about your product or service is more likely to generate the kind of response you desire.

You could also count the dollar value of increased business or the amount of goodwill and recognition toward the value of the publicist's services.

The dollar value you receive in media exposure is usually several times the amount you pay the publicist, and a properly executed promotional campaign will continue to yield business dollars far into the future.

The Publicist's Fee

A publicist usually charges either by the hour or by the project. He or she is paid for time spent interviewing you, brainstorming your image and approach, originating appropriate promotional materials, selecting the proper media outlets, and following up with phone calls.

Often, depending on the publicist's professional profile, the hourly rate is a sizable amount. Keep in mind, however, that the publicist will not partake in either the short- or the long-term increase in your business. And if you are observant you will also benefit by learning a great deal more about the public-relations process from the publicist and will be able to use that information to your advantage long after the publicist departs.

You can keep the publicist's billable hours down by being prepared for your meetings. Reading this book will give you an idea of what to expect and how to organize your thinking.

Some publicists work by taking a percentage of earned results. However, that kind of arrangement often leads to disputes or at least to the dissolution of relationships. A clearly defined hourly fee or project fee should be agreed upon in writing. Of course, as with any contracted service, you should have the written agreement approved by your business attorney.

How to Find a Publicist

As with any other service you contract to use, it is best to seek a professional in the field. A good bet is the recommendation of a friend. If you elect to find a publicist from the yellow pages of your telephone book, certainly ask for references and call those references to check the person's track record.

Most publicists specialize in specific areas. For example, one person might assist small businesses while others specialize in restaurants, authors, sports events, or nonprofits.

The key factors in a successful campaign are mutual comfort, trust, and respect for each other. A publicist must like you in order to spend hours on the telephone pitching your story. It is rather an intimate relationship in that you must trust your publicist to help you "invent" yourself. In fact, that is what you are doing: you are inventing the public you. Therefore, it is essential that the person you choose as a publicist approach the task with a similar value system and point of view. A publicist with diametrically opposed views will sooner or later be at odds with you.

Any agreement should have a cancellation clause for terminating the publicist's services. Also, you can require regular meetings and a weekly or monthly update of what is being accomplished. If, for example, the publicist has been working with you for six months and you haven't seen one iota of results, it's time to find another publicist.

Results

A publicist promises to execute tasks aimed at generating media interest in you and your product or service. However, there is no way of predicting or ensuring inclusion in specific electronic or print media, although in your agreement and plan you can target selected outlets. Publicists who promise they can get you on this or that show on a specific date are suspect. Publicists who guarantee they can garner a certain dollar figure of free exposure are suspect.

Seeking publicity involves a risk. But if you've chosen to be in business, you're accustomed to taking risks; risk taking is essential to creating and sustaining business growth. It is a greater risk *not* to analyze your promotional needs and fully exercise your PR Power. Adequate promotion is an essential factor in continued business success.

20

Assessing the Progress of
Your Promotional Campaign

Public relations is an imperfect science. No one is capable of telling you specifically which media appearances or articles will get the results you desire. Those who call themselves experts will pretend to know just the right strategy to improve customer sales. The truth, however, is that no one can accurately predict just what promotional campaign will bring the results you desire. Each case requires an individually tailored promotional plan with individual measures of success.

In public relations, experience is the best teacher and observation the supreme tutor. Observe media response to your invitations and proposals. Observe audience response to your presentations. Master the nuances of expression, changing your message to include or exclude certain information to get the desired response. You will elicit differing responses when you hard-sell your product, when you soft-sell, and when you don't sell at all. You must discern differences in the levels of audience response and react appropriately.

Measuring Results

The ultimate measure of a successful promotional campaign is whether it brings you increased sales. Don't get caught up in the flurry of becoming a media darling and forget the bottom line: earning money. If you have been exerting your PR power and getting little response from new customers, it's time to analyze your campaign. If your promotional campaign is flourishing but your sales volume isn't, you are delivering the wrong message. Getting on the air and enjoying print but with little or no positive response means you have not yet found the words to express to the public the value of what you have to offer.

In Chapter Two we discussed ways of measuring the effectiveness of your media campaign in terms of the publicity you receive and the sales that publicity generates. Now take a close look at those costs and benefits and find the weak spots in your campaign that may be causing you to waste time and money. Be realistic and hard-nosed in your analysis.

Using the number of people estimated to have seen your campaign, calculate what percentage are buying your product or service. Are you just entertaining the Lookee Lous and window-shoppers of the world? Is your message strong enough to get into the pocketbooks of audiences you reach? Knowing whether you're giving the right spiel to the wrong audience or hyping your wares on the wrong show is an important key to finding a solution to your response problems.

Sometimes a minor adjustment in your strategy can make a phenomenal difference. Experiment with your presentation. You should also alter your approach so you appeal to a different kind of customer than you have in the past. For example, if you are presently promoting your financial seminars to young professionals try aiming your pitch to the working family of four with limited income.

You can also move your message along the scale between hard- and soft-sell, adjusting until it works. Pick an aspect of your business that you've previously ignored and emphasize it. Control your experiment (change only one factor at a time) so you can get precise data on the success of your new strategy.

Changing Promotional Campaigns

Sometimes it is difficult to give up a cherished idea, to declare that you have failed, and to seek a new way. However, if you view that failure as one step up the ladder toward success, it becomes simply a learning experience. If you are to conduct an effective public-relations campaign you must be willing to see those aspects of your strategy that are doomed, to cut your losses, and to move ahead. Time wasted in lamenting what might have been is time when you are not being booked on your favorite talk shows or reaching the audiences who will buy your product or service.

When should you make a change in your promotional campaign? After you think you've had enough of wasting your time and energy with activity that isn't paying off!

It generally takes about six months to determine whether your publicity campaign is working. However, if three months have gone by after your last mailing and you have received no media response, or when people you call are still unresponsive, it's time to abandon that program.

If you have a campaign you believed to be creative and effective that is actually a dismal failure, give it up. Start anew. Pretend you are your own client. Take a fresh approach, find a new angle, and test your ideas on friends. On the other hand, if you are waging a campaign that is building name recognition you believe will pay off in the future but that is not yielding direct sales right now, consider augmenting it rather than abandoning it.

Trial and error are what will guide you to the serene state of confidence in which you become certain that the way you are promoting yourself is right. Your PR power will energize you as you develop your unique style. To reach that stage, you must be willing to risk criticism, to dare to be different, to explore options that previously you might not have had the nerve to consider.

Public relations is a living, breathing process that continuously requires care and feeding of new ideas and infusions of energy. It is not a structured formula but rather a flexible system applying a variety of techniques. Mastering these techniques yields the exciting ability to motivate large numbers of people and to tap into the "power of the press." This power becomes yours when you have the faith, creative imagination, energy, and courage to claim it. That's PR power. Your PR power.

Index

telemarketing: elements of, 67–69; handling difficult situations, 76–77; pitfalls, 74–75; stages of the conversation, 69–73; techniques, 77

Television Factbook, 57

travel agency, 182

T.V. Publicity Outlets, 57

upholsterer, 182

Ulrich's International Periodicals Directory, 154

veterinarian, 37, 39, 41

video store, 118, 182

weight-reduction consultant, 182, 184

what-if scenarios. *See* interview, "what-if?"

wire service, 60–61

Working Press of the Nation, 57, 154

writer's block, 44

yoga instructor, 184